DON'T CURSE YOUR
Wedding Bed
BEFORE YOU SAY
'*I Do*'

BOOK ENDORSEMENTS

This book is truly heartfelt and speaks from the very heart of the author. It expresses how faith in God proves that no matter how bad your situation may be or the level that the enemy has reduced you to, "Little becomes much when placed in the Master's hands." We commend our daughter, Tara, on the work God has blessed and called her to do in order to draw people to Him. God Bless You. We are proud and always humbled.

— Mr. Andrew I. D. and Diane Harris, (My Parents).

This book serves as an excellent resource for any individual striving to live life to the fullest. It is filled with lively examples from past experiences and reveals the power of faith, prayer, and perseverance. Every individual who has "faith the size of a mustard seed" should have a copy on hand. It truly blessed our hearts!

— Mr. Brent T. & Aleashia L. Brandon, MBA, LRT/CTRS

God uses author Tara White to expose and explain how God causes "all things to work together for the good of them that love God and are called according to His purpose" (Romans 8:28). This book is a compilation of how family dynamics, social experiences, cultural influences, personal life events, painful childhood experiences, unexpected people, and divine intervention all interrelate and impact the transition and stability in marriage and relationships. This material is a must-read for all ages, as it challenges readers to evaluate sensitive relational issues and embrace relational resolve from both a psychological and theological perspective.

— Pastor R. Thomas Wyatt Jr. & Minister Tina R. Wyatt, M.A., M. Div., LPC

This book is genuine and heartfelt. Tara shares her heart and experiences to reach out to help others. *Don't Curse The Wedding Bed Before You Say I Do* is inspirationally written to help others triumph over life's mistakes, trials, and tribulations through Jesus Christ. This book will capture your heart, soul, and mind. You will be blessed and encouraged by this book.

— Pastor Rickey and Peggy H. Johnson

For those of you who are seeking to find a gateway to your deliverance, we dare you to open your mind and hearts to *Don't Curse Your Wedding Bed Before You Say I Do*. No matter if you are young or old, lost or saved, this is a compelling work ready to be planted in fertile soil. One day, the Refiner will come back, and He desires to see his reflection (Malachi 3:1-3). This book challenges you to step into the Refiner's fire and allow it to purify you to a priceless value.

— Ministers Michael A. & Lasheka L. White

This book has inspired us to reflect and use it as a practical guide toward transforming our life toward spiritual fulfillment. It will be useful to assist others toward achieving their maximum potential of which he or she is capable of achieving. It also reflects a practical spiritual guide toward self, relationships, love, family, life's purpose, and spiritual eternity. Please enjoy the shared experiences from this book. Tara, continue your journey of love and inspiring others.

— Mr. William T. & Andrais L. Brandon, Entrepreneurs

If you are someone who is still wrestling with hurt that gnaws you to the bone, this book is a must-read for you. Read it and begin your journey to spiritual cleansing and renewal.

— W. J. Kennedy, Retired Educator

In this unvarnished, hard-hitting, frank and tough-loving truth; Tara, a very brave soul deals with issues and not images that most people dare not mention. Her wisdom and honesty aims at shining a light into the dark corners of every heart to guide every reader through a process of purification. This book will help every bachelor and spinster become free from the bondage of sexuality!

— Rev Ronnie Nsubuga, Bestselling Author of A Legacy of Choices, and President, Tender Mercies Foundation.

DON'T CURSE YOUR
Wedding Bed
BEFORE YOU SAY
'I Do'

TARA WHITE

WORD**PUBLISHERS**

CANADA • NEW YORK • MARYLAND • WASHINGTON, D.C.

1st Edition 2010 © Tara White

For more information write to:

417 W. 17th Street

Spencer, North Carolina 28159

JOIN THE MOVEMENT: www.weddingbed.net

Or

Word Publishers

1.888.345.WORD

www.wpublishers.com

For Worldwide Distribution

Printed in Canada

ISBN: 10#: 0-9819837-2-3

13#: 978-0-9819837-2-1

Library of Congress Cataloging-in-Publication Data:

An application to register this book for Cataloging has been submitted to the Library of Congress.

1 2 3 4 5 6 7 8 9 10 / 09 08 07 06 05

DEDICATION

This book is dedicated to my husband and my daughter, Bird, the loves of my life, who rode the rollercoaster ride called life with me and continue to love and bless me daily. You inspired me to make a difference. You inspire others to get back on track when something happens along the way. You inspired in me many of God's proclamations that He had planned for my well-being and not my calamity.

Obviously, going through the riptide, it seemed like I was worse for wear, yet you two inspired me to fully embrace "I do" not by simply saying "I did it" but by gaining the strength to maintain my efforts when times got tough.

ACKNOWLEDGEMENT

J oseph was a dreamer. In Genesis chapter 37, the Bible illustrates how God blessed Joseph with favor and how Joseph was determined to trust God and dream, no matter what negative situation he found himself in. Please allow me to say a word of thanks to those who have helped me to maintain my dream through extreme circumstances.

First and foremost, I thank God for choosing me to birth this message. Despite all the challenges I faced while working on this project, God gave me the grace and dignity to walk through them. His grace and mercy are the reason for my very existence and the reason why this book exists. I love Him more than anything!

Tito J. White: Before I was born, God knew exactly what I would need. He created you specifically for me. You are always in my corner, and you always have my back. Your input and encouragement throughout this entire project blessed me immensely.

Andrew and Diane Harris: You are the best parents this side of Heaven. You continually encouraged me to reach for the stars and go after my dreams. Thank you for believing in me and being there for me throughout this project. You poured love into me despite how things may have looked.

Tianca D. White: Thank you for loving me unconditionally. You have been a blessing to me during this project and taught me that I could truly learn a lot from a child if I simply listen.

Thank you, Aleashia L. Brandon, for all the late nights you stayed up with me, working, reading, discussing, laughing, yawning, and e-mailing. You blessed me by simply being there when I needed you.

Deborah Gross: You cannot put a price tag on kindness. As I traveled from N.C. to Maryland working on the book deal, you embraced me and my dream and allowed us a place in your heart as well as your home. Your generosity is unmatched.

Janice Hall: You have always been the older sister I never had. Thank you for believing in me, encouraging me to follow this dream, and for being a listening ear when I needed it. Your faith walk inspires me to stand.

I also appreciate my entire Baltimore family. I hold you so dearly.

Jean B. Kennedy: Your encouragement and listening ear were truly a blessing to me while I worked on this project. God uses you to impart wisdom and bless others. Our spirits are truly connected. Thank you so much for your input.

Minister LaSheka L. White: You are the midwife who helped birth this dream. You were praying, fasting, crying, shouting, and encouraging, whatever you had to do, to get me to "PUSH", even down to the most difficult moment, the last push. You forced me to produce.

Mary F. Davis: A spiritual mother who taught me to have NO fear... and that all of my troubles and worries are to be given to God. I will never forget the words she always told me in my times of trouble: "You have no worries; God is still on the Throne." Rest In Peace, Mother Davis.

Bishop Phillip M. Davis and Pastor Cynthia L. Davis: Your ministry teaches me that, with God, "I can leap over walls," (2 Samuel 22:30). Thank you so much for your prayers and your shining example of faith.

Pastor R. Thomas Wyatt Jr. and Minister Tina Wyatt:

Your ministry teaches me humility, obedience, and focus, despite what the circumstances may be. As a result, I can now say for myself, "I know what He told me." Thank you for your prayers and your acts of love.

Pastor Rickey Johnson and Peggy Johnson: Your ministry teaches me true courage and steadfastness. You boldly proclaim God's Word, and your love for Him and His people is evident. Thank you for your prayers and kindness.

Rev. Ronnie P. Nsubuga: I thank God you have an ear to hear what the Spirit is saying. You embraced this project and worked diligently, compassionately, and selflessly. Your agenda is to bless others with the absence of shame or pretense. Thank you for giving me a chance with this project.

Many others have been pivotal to my spiritual growth and

development and have taught me the value of living in the Spirit. They have enabled me to make decisions in line with God's plan for my life. I am deeply indebted to those who stood by my side when I least deserved it. I especially thank Duane Harvey, Barbara Ruff, Minister Diane Robinson, and Mrs. Sherry Russell, who taught me early on about the blessing of prayer and agreement.

Master Damian A. Brandon: I will never forget my nephew's wonderful reminder to me during the time of this project: "You have to have courage!"

I would like to thank Rev. Ronnie P. Nsubuga and Duane Harvey for helping me bring the best out of me.

CONTENTS

FOREWORD

By Min. LaSheka L. White

Many times, as we journey through life's experiences, we often find ourselves stuck or paralyzed in the moment. For the Word said in Jeremiah 1:5, before we were formed in our mother's womb, He knew us. So what does that mean? He knew our parents even when they were abusive, and he still decided to plant us there. He knew our spouses when we were led to unite as one, even when the rage of violence and control just so happened to take over. He knew that we would use drugs and alcohol to medicate the wounds of rape and molestation. He knew that we would harbor a life of looking for love in all the wrong places. He even knew that the life of walking death would try to rob us of our destiny.

The amazing thought I like to keep close to my heart is that He also knew that the life ahead would be full of eternal treasures.

The journey of life sometimes causes us to visualize dreams that never appear to come true. What little girl does not dream of one day walking down the aisle and marrying the perfect man, Mr. Right? However, due to her horrific past, she is ashamed and embarrassed of the journey she has walked. So, instead of embracing and accepting her dream, she lives in the shadow of the dream.

For many years, Christians have been bound by and ashamed of their sins and life experiences of the present and past. The time has come when Christians need to take off all the garments of life which weigh us down in our journey. We are to become naked and unashamed. From generation to generation, we have allowed the enemy's tricks and schemes to produce powder-puff Christians and to curse the very bed in which we lie in night after night.

In Genesis 2:25, Adam and Eve were the first example of believers who roamed the Garden of Eden, living a pure life with no sin. Then Satan, the author of sin, convinced Eve that she was missing out on something wonderful. It became the curse of mankind. It amazes me how the very thing that we think we cannot live without becomes the very thing that delivers us to the pathway of our death.

As you began to turn the pages of *Don't Curse Your Wedding Bed Before You Say I Do*, I challenge you to surrender your soul to the safest place in the whole world: The will of God the Creator, the one who knew your journey before you started it. He desires to smell the purest aroma of your soul, even the broken places where He desires to "Shabar" (Hebrew for birth) your destiny.

The choice is yours: a cursed bed or a bed of restoration. I hearken you to bathe in the cleansing blood of Jesus Christ instead of the horrific blood of your old sins. This book is designed to convey healing into your life, and it is also a call for Christians to model a testimonial life of transparency, one that has been covered with the blood of Jesus Christ, with victory on every end.

PREFACE

If you are a teen who thinks that you are ready for a committed relationship, whether you're ready to take it to the next level or not, this book is for you.

If you're single and wondering if there is truly such a thing as Mr. or Mrs. Right, then read this book.

If you are wondering about the phrase, '. . . happily ever after', this book will delightfully fulfill your dream.

If you're married and seeking help with a troubled relationship, this book will more than ease the pain.

If you're happily married and simply seeking Godly wisdom to stay that way, this book is heaven-sent.

If you're divorced and not sure if you will ever love again

or commit to another lasting relationship, this book is divinely-designed for you.

Lastly, if you're a man and you want to learn all that you can, don't read this book and weep; read it as a much-needed treat.

Let me stipulate that the forthright and poignant retelling of my life is designed to awaken the sleeping giant within each potential reader. At times, you might be further propelled to find out what god-awful experiences this writer has had to endure and to what magnitude these experiences have shaped the character of this person. I put forth my experiences so that you can compare and contrast them with yourself and others.

Chapter One

YOUR MEASURE

*"Change is disturbing when it is done to us,
exhilarating when it is done by us."*

— (Rosabeth Moss Kanter, Harvard Business School)

You're measured as a workman
　By just the things you do
When there's nobody looking
　And no one knows but you.
Your only real value
　Is what you think and say
When no one ever hears it
　And sham is stripped away

Your power is determined
　By simply what is found

To be your code of honor
  When no one is around
Your character is founded
  Without the slightest doubt
On just your course of action
  When no one will find out.

You're rated — just remember
  By only what is true —
No matter what the seeming
  Of all you say and do
For Truth cannot be covered,
  And so we stand or fall
Just by the fundamentals
  Of what we are — that's all.

Sidney J. Burgoyne

We live in a world where people, situations, and things relate to one another in some way, shape, or form. As you proceed through this text, keep this in mind: Be Committed.

I say that because this book of discourse contains truths that are discomforting to acknowledge but that, in essence, are at the heart of the matter: Relationships. This book is designed to help redefine your relationships.

Moreover, this book does more than share the highs and lows of committed relationships. It is not meant to be portrayed in the wrong light. It distills valuable insight that will enable you to see people in a much different light. In short, it will be a delightful awakening or reawakening.

As delightful as that may be, things often get lost in the sauce. At times, each of us has difficulty separating the wheat from the chaff (distinguishing the wanted from the unwanted). Again, this book will bring about the recurring motif of 'I wish I knew then what I know now.'

In the grand scheme of things, life can be a tussle — a rough and tumble struggle. We don't often heap praise about the struggle, but boy-oh-boy do we praise the triumph. Still, as quiet as it's kept, the struggle continues. A day in the life of each of us would reflect this truth. Still, however it goes, we all want continuity. We all want to have a place on an unbroken course. That is easier said than done. In fact, life will turn us any which way but loose if it can, until the true course of our life is impressed upon us.

The thing that I want to impress upon your mind and empower your spirit with is this profound truth: Life is full of ambiguities, meaning that it is susceptible to multiple interpretations. In other words, there are many twists and turns, as well as cultural, financial, emotional, spiritual, psychological, and other barriers that we must break through.

We tend to forget that we are one of many. Yes, we are individuals, but no, we are not alone. That appears to be a contradiction. If it is, it is a living contradiction. More importantly, it is a profoundly parabolic truth. Remember that there are two great stories of life: leaving home and coming back.

This book is designed to reconnect you with something that you may have missed or perhaps lost. If that's the case, it can be found again.

It is also about United Souls meant to empower each other. The question is: What is empowerment? It may be defined as the means by which individuals, groups, and/or communities become able to take control of their circumstances and achieve their own goals, thereby being able to work toward helping themselves and others to maximize the quality of their lives.

Seasons of Life

Have you ever listened to Vivaldi's *The Four Seasons*? This is a set of four violin concertos by Antonio Vivaldi. Composed in 1723, *The Four Seasons* is Vivaldi's best-known work and is among the most popular pieces of Baroque music. It is known for triumphant changes that reflect the seasons of life.

Even though I live in North Carolina, I am very aware of how seasons affect nature and people all over the world. In nature, a tree goes through an interesting cycle. In spring, after enduring a harsh winter, a tree starts to blossom. In the summer, it is in full bloom. In the fall, its leaves radiate different beautiful colors before they fall to the ground. In the winter, the leafless tree fights through until it has completed the full cycle.

Our lives mirror and match those of trees. In the spring and summer, we shine while awaiting our season of change. Autumn reflects the pruning and displacement we all go through from time to time. In the winter, the season of our discontent (dissatisfaction or restless aspiration for improvement), we are made aware that spring is just around the corner if we can get through the harshness surrounding our lives at the time.

True enough, we all have weathered through rough seasons during our growing pains. However, in the midst of whatever season you are in, simply realize that there is always hope right around the corner. To really clear your mind, I beseech you to open yourself up to enlightenment.

Stumbling Blocks or Building Blocks?

I and many other people have let our pasts become stumbling blocks to our future progress. We have fallen into seasons of despair for a variety of reasons: Broken relationships, fractured friendships, sunken treasures, shattered dreams, et cetera. These momentary setbacks can become long-term if we don't find truth and reconciliation.

Some people don't really understand themselves at all. Some become so invested in their own righteousness that they call themself "Captain of my own ship". They inflate or enlarge themselves. Don't get me wrong; we all are prone to self-righteousness, but some take it to the highest degree.

Still, some see themselves in a different light. They portray themselves as victims even when they are doing the victimizing. All I can say for now to these types is that there is no gain without pain. As a North Carolinian, I can rightfully assert that if the homegrown Michael Jordan had not overcome failing at first at basketball in high school, his name would not be worthy of special mention now. That is why I want us to move beyond playing the "Blame Game", in which we excuse ourselves by finding fault in others or blaming our faults on others. This type of antic alone can be a hindrance or a stumbling block for us. In full disclosure, it hindered me for years.

Having stated that, let me emphasize that many buckle under pressure because they let stress overshadow them and make them shiver with fear. That downtrodden feeling makes them want to run and hide. In such a lopsided situation, many of us feel lonely and isolated. Our self-worth feels depleted and our minds become darkened with despair.

But is all lost?

The beautiful thing, like the sun on a dark and cloudy day, is that hope springs eternal when we realize that light can shine through darkness. If you truly want to see the light, keep in mind that for every setback there is a solution. Remember that, if you truly want to see the light.

I know firsthand that hope abounds.

In my present situation, my wisdom grows whether I am around strangers or acquaintances, because I have been fortunate to be able to look back over my life with honest and prayerful reflection. As a result, my evaporated hopes have been transformed into distinct possibilities, such as reaching out to those who have gone through or may go through similar trials and triumphs in their lives.

I'll give you an up-close-and-personal example: I was blessed with the gift of song. I was told from the age of six that my singing ability was heaven-sent, and that was my building block. Yet from ages six to twenty-six, I was paralyzed with fear until my spirit was broken and I had no confidence in my singing ability. That was my stumbling block. I shut down.

My truth and reconciliation came once I realized that I was my own worst enemy. In the last thirteen years, I've opened up again and now sing as if I had never fallen down in the first place. Thank God, it seeped into my soul that what I thought I lost was not lost at all.

In reality, what I had once deemed as a stumbling block has actually become one of my building blocks as I share my gift of song with others.

Does the same hold true for you?

Vicissitudes

Life is full of changes in one way or another. Life is full of alterations in nature or human affairs. To give you an example, someone shared with me their fascination with driving on Highway 68 in Maryland. They loved seeing how man travels through nature.

They saw a place called Sideling Hill, where highway construction cut through a mountain, exposing all that was inside.

That example made me think of change, mainly of the self, which always interacts with others. Whether we are accepted or rejected by others determines how our lives are shaped. Still, in understanding how the self is transformed like the Sideling Hill, we can begin to understand that we all go through vicissitudes upon life's highway.

I share that piece of life's pie in order to share another piece of humble pie with you.

It dawned on me during my early years that we live in a world of justice and injustice. I mainly learned it through negotiation. I learned how to negotiate with others at home and in school. I, in effect, played the 'give and take' game. It made a firm impression on me that sometimes people take more than they give. It created conflicts that, at times, could be resolved easier than others.

It was at this point in my life when I realized that being a problem solver is similar to being a detective. You have to search for hidden things. Likewise, you have to not only exercise your own sense of power; you have to hand whatever or whomever over to a higher power. It takes wielding power to bring about justice. Of course, I was searching for more answers. Naturally, I turned to my parents. In simple terms, I saw my father as a provider and my mother as a caregiver. I saw them as two peas but not in the same pod. Disturbingly, I saw that their approach to conflict was more geared toward win/lose.

Let me be frank in declaring that I was not empowered to trust my ability to handle my social situations. The phrase, 'It's my way or the highway' was being etched into my mind. Therefore, I saw that power comes in many different forms. I made a mental note of that, because, as time would reveal, I would use and abuse power while being used and abused by power. That fortunate and unfortunate reality of life is a part of what makes you and me changeable, because we must be altered by vicissitudes — like it or not.

Empowering Anthem

More than ever, I understand the importance of bonding, especially in terms of relationships. I realize that bonding between people, situations, and things is a lot easier said than done. Upon reflection, I realized that in the '70s it was a lot easier to bond with people. In the '80s, it was easier to bond with people and situations. In the '90s, things were easier to bond with than people. Nowadays, I see that many prefer things first, situations second, and people third. It is as if things are more important than people.

That stated, let me ask: Have you ever made a change in your life that influenced yourself and others? How effective was that change?

The key principle underlying this notion of *effective change* is empowerment. To be empowered is to be made aware of the power of change that resides within you. Without question, I know this now more than ever.

To become empowered means to be given the breadth and depth of knowledge to empower others. In other words, it is a *quid pro quo* (an equal exchange or substitution). Two more phrases speak to this same point: 'Exchange is no robbery,' and, 'Something for something.' Thus we cannot easily dismiss this empowering term. Instead, it should be made clear that by empowering an individual you give them the power to transform their quality of life. I sincerely add that because I know for an astonishing fact that, all too often, others believe in us more than we believe in ourselves. To make this painstakingly clear, I know many people who don't believe they can do this or that until someone encourages them to take the first step.

Remember the old proverb: Give a man a fish and he will eat for a day; teach him how to fish and he will eat for a lifetime. This is something for something.

Before I proceed, let me ask: How does this impact you? If it helps, please realize that many of us have taken the wrong path due to childhood mishaps, teenage misdirection, or young adult vision quests until someone stepped in to help and redirect us.

If the same holds true for you, you can make the difference if you confront the downward spiral that you, a loved one, or a beloved friend or foe has encountered. You can help them help themselves if you don't assume an air of superiority or lord their errors over them.

Before I proceed further, I want to encourage you to understand that all of us live social lives. Many of us are socialized by folkways (a custom or belief common to members of a society or culture) and mores *(mor-rays* — societal norms and customs of a particular social group that come to be regarded as essential to survival). We also all come from a neighborhood, walk of life, or circle that marinates and makes a firm impression on our lives. So even if we wanted to be *laissez-faire,* we can't just shrug that off as "What will be, will be."

We have to understand that our lives are full of social interactions. In the midst of these is a dynamic called 'social power', the influence a person exerts on others. For example, a police car with lights flashing and siren blaring while driving up behind you exerts a legitimate sense of power over you.

Subsequently, as relationships become more established, they make stern impressions, whether good or bad. The thing we cannot miss is that it is in our best interest to empower others. To understand the full scope of it, realize that it will help you in the home and community if that is your calling. Empowerment as a *tour de force* makes you actively involved in the decision-making process. Don't forget that it is a process, meaning that it is an ongoing journey that will enrich your life as you enrich others. Lastly, it will make you a change maker. Therefore, I implore you to go there and make that change happen!

Let's Stay Together

Speaking of change makers, let me share these lyrics with you:

Let's stay together . . . whether times are good or bad or happy or sad.

— Al Green

Let me also tell a monumental story that shows the dynamic of togetherness:

The 2000 Olympics in Sydney, Australia produced a variety of interesting stories. The one that significantly impacts the 'together' motif is the story of Laura Wilkinson, a platform diver.

After the semifinals, she was in fifth place. She went out to perform her fourth out of five dives, determined to do her most difficult one. Just before she climbed to the diving platform, she stated, "Do it for Hilary." She was recalling her friend and former teammate, Hilary Grivich, who had died in a car accident in 1997. Then, to top it all off, she stated, "I can do all things through Christ, who strengthens me."

She went on to nail her gold medal and triumphantly showcased to all of us that we can pull inspiration from a deep well if we are mindful that we are not alone, even when it seems as though we are not going down an easy road.

I share that story because it hits a familiar chord with me personally. God allows trials and tribulations to draw his children closer to him. True enough, I've had many 'uh-oh' moments in my life. At times, it makes me teary-eyed when I think about how my negative emotions morphed into positive ones and took me into God's presence. I want to stay there forever.

Both Near and Far

Our lives are filled with many social dynamics as we navigate through a maze of class, culture, race, religion, and geography, only to name a few. By understanding these dynamics, we can perceive why things go awry and astray as often as they do: Because during many seasons, there is a germination process in which the seed bursts through the soil to reveal the destined plant.

If we are honest, things seem both near and far at the same time. Have you ever sent a message of love to someone who you thought loved you, only to receive a look of disdain?

My point in bringing this up is that we belong in a world of interpersonal relationships that are reminiscent and reflective of our background. That is why we need to understand and realize how social class affects our response to the larger social world. If you think about it, the world is tribal or clannish in a variety of different ways. One of the most dominant ways in America is through social class. It has a tight grip on families to the point where we are all conditioned by it, whether we accept it or reject it.

A friend shared a *New York Times* article with me, which read: "Class is still a powerful force in American life. Over the past three decades, it has come to play a greater, not lesser, role in important ways. At a time when education matters more than ever, success in school remains linked tightly to class. At a time when the country is increasingly integrated racially, the rich are isolating themselves more and more. At a time of extraordinary advances in medicine, class differences in health and lifespan are wide and appear to be widening."

To bring that article into full view, we must accept a truism of American life. In America, people's wealth and social status fall into the middle class, which tends to be the acceptable norm. It is what most people strive to be, and those who have it strive not to lose it. It is a social class system like the middle of the up escalator; it can go up but it doesn't want to go back down. It deviates or goes from zone to zone depending on social relations. Sometimes the relations get personal; other times they are general; occasionally they get intimate. Nevertheless, it is what many aspire to be. Still, whether you are rich, poor, or in-between, we all face challenges. Our social-class mindset tends to affect our child rearing, home life, and even public way of being.

As influential as social class is in our lives, it is closely associated with culture, which are the enduring behaviors, ideas, attitudes, and traditions shared by a large group of people and transmitted from one generation to another.

Keep these dynamics in mind, because they are always both near and far away.

Diverse, I, See

I encourage you to grasp the fact that we live in a world of many diversities, cultures, religions, and races. Naturally, as human history will show, cultures are not always at peace with each other. Not only do love and hate go hand-in-hand, love and war are Siamese twins.

There are people from Japan, India, Latin America, and other countries who move from their respective countries to places that give them the best upswing. In their new place, they are torn by the new things they encounter.

We really need to grasp this, because we all face countercultural changes that force us to adapt to new surroundings. To some degree, we all know how to put on a fake smile and go with the flow, but it's deeper than that.

In North Carolina, as well as all over the United States, people understand that their comfort zone will be shaken and expanded like silly putty. Yet when they move to these places, they should understand that their children will want to learn the new culture and may not fully follow the old culture. This is where the tug-of-war begins, especially if the parents love and believe in their old culture so much.

When someone comes from a different country, they should know that they cannot follow their culture or religion the way they did in their country. They may desire to do so but might not find it entirely feasible. It is important to realize that our world contains different cultures and diversities, and we have to find peace when these cultures clash.

IF

In nearly every imaginable predicament, 'if' will show up on the scene. It is a conditional word that makes its presence felt. For example, "I can order the food *if* I have the money."

I bring this up to illustrate the startling fact that a lot of our life requires consequential choices. Frankly, we often take our 'if' choices for granted. Because I have come to value my thinking side in relation to the reacting side of me, I am more aware of 'if' than ever. It is worthy of considerable mention because there will be a variety of situations, conditions, or circumstances that will utilize our decision-making abilities. If we fail to see the consequences, we can make one decision that leaves a dire lifelong affect. For example, someone told me the story of a young lady who, in a desire to get back at her less-than-desirable husband, thought, *If I sleep with another man, I can hurt my husband.* She got trapped in a torrid three-way love affair that sent a rippling effect throughout her family. She lost custody of her two children, and, due to her tubes being tied, she couldn't have any more.

Today she says, "If I hadn't done that, I would be better off." I concur with her on many levels, as I will showcase throughout my disclosure. However, the ifs that permeate my life show me in full force that the proverbial words of knowledge, wisdom, and understanding are underrated. For example, I thought, *If I simply mirror his behavior, I will be just as good as him, never outdone or outmatched.*

Odd Girl(s) Out

Although I am the centerpiece of this book, I have opened it up for others to share interesting reflections, anecdotes, and much more. Some people to whom I reached out had read *Odd Girl Out* by Rachel Simmons, which states that girls have "a hidden culture of silent and indirect aggression." I will share others' reflections on this piece.

In the book, Molly was discussing her parents' divorce and her mother's physical handicap. She said, "Because, you know, everybody has two parents and I don't."

18

A schoolteacher from the Midwest shared this excerpt:

"This hit me on both a personal and professional level. I was a child of divorce in the late '60s. At the time, although increasing, this was an uncommon occurrence. Even more unusual was the fact that my father had custody of all five of us. We were coddled and shown compassion and caring by the neighbors in our little ethnic enclave in Cleveland.

"All that changed in 1970, when we moved to Bay Village with our grandparents and father. This was the land of *Leave it to Beaver;* the people had perfect little houses (with perfect little lawns), perfect little families, and perfect little lives. I had no mom; my dad worked a factory job from six in the afternoon to six in the morning, and all I had was my grandparents. We did not fit in.

"I remember that all my friends were constantly going to the mall or movies with their mothers and I never could. Not only did I not have a mom, most of the time I did not have a dad. My grandparents were not physically able or emotionally willing to invest in us.

"Professionally, I deal with the issues of divorce and family separation on a daily basis. I cannot tell you how my heart aches for those children who are separated from their families for whatever reason, especially from their mothers. I think your mother is an integral part of who you are, and to not have one as an active part of your life is simply heartbreaking. When my mother dies, I hope and pray to God that I have the spiritual faith, not the emotional will, to actually attend her funeral."

I know what it is like to feel clueless in situations like this. The above reflection is heart-wrenching to me on some level, but it's mainly an eye-opening reminder. I sometimes forget that parenting is more than making your presence known. It involves teaching social and emotional coping skills. For me, social skills involve conversations, cooperating, sharing viewpoints, and more. Emotional skills are the abilities to effectively communicate, to keep your frustrations down, to exercise self-control, and more.

So many things swoop into my mind regarding parenting, considering I have one child and one sister. As I will chronicle, my parents were present and although they worked a lot at the same time; they were there. They bring to mind Ecclesiastes 3:1 "To everything there is a season, a time for every purpose under Heaven."

Chapter Two

PERCEPTION IS EVERYTHING

"Great minds discuss ideas,
Average minds discuss events,
Small minds discuss people."

Anonymous

Laissez-faire

I am perturbed by many signs of the times. One is this noninterference in the affairs of others, or being *laissez-faire*. I'm sure that you, like me, hear people say, "Let them do their own thing." Trust me when I tell you that it's a trap when we think and say things of that nature.

We don't want to come across as a busybody prying into people's lives, but, nonetheless, we want to make our intentions clear. However, 'coming across' and 'appearing to be' are two different things, though they both involve dealing with how you see people and how they see you.

When you 'come across as', you appear to have a particular character or attitude. You take a decisive approach, even if you do it in a skillful manner. For example, I came across as a know-it-all youngster at times only to wish I had never done so.

On the other side, 'appear to be' talks about how others perceive you. Many of us know people who appear to be one way yet are another. They don't want to ruffle feathers (annoy or irritate someone). They act as if they want the wrong kind of approval.

As a person who looked for love in all the wrong places and faces, I could have done abundantly well if my so-called loved ones had mindfully steered me in the right direction. Instead, many labeled me as a lost cause rather than as a worthy adversary.

Case in point: Bear in mind that Abraham Lincoln proclaimed Harriet Beecher Stowe 'The author of the Civil War' for her book, *Uncle Tom's Cabin*. It galvanized the hearts and minds of her fellow countrymen and women. If she had never been exposed to the horrible reality of slavery, would she have been *laissez-faire* and ignored it?

We are socially influenced whether we admit it or not. It is a key component of our social behavior. We constantly interact with others. When we accept that everyone wants to be loved and accepted on some level, we become much wiser. We must realize that people, through apparent love and acceptance, become too selfish. Interestingly, altruism is a behavior that reflects unselfish concern for the welfare of others. Never forget that selfishness and unselfishness are continually vying for optimum attention.

To reinforce how much conformity plays a major role in social influence, I will share an anecdote that highlights a bevy of issues: A reporter was working on a piece about the triumvirate winners out of seventeen high schools. She turned to the police department's records for information; they indicated that students physically attacked teachers, security guards, and each other, engaging in spitting, pushing, hitting, and punching.

Alarmingly, these students, both male and female, used multiple weapons, combination locks, metal yardsticks, brass knuckles, razor blades, knives, and guns. These kids were not afraid to use mob violence to destructive ends. Several reports showed more than ten girls at a time beating up one solitary girl; there was also a large fistfight involving between twenty and thirty girls. There was another fight involving almost two hundred kids.

The reporter's article gave detailed accounts of many violent acts being played out between these schools. Individually, each school report indicated much of the same. At one school, there were incidents ranging from vicious threats to three-gang fights. One girl attacked another with an eyebrow archer, while another spat in a teacher's face. A teacher and a principal were left with broken bones after altercations with students. There were several large fights, the most heinous of which involved students throwing snowballs at handicapped students. At another school, a flying chair knocked out a principal and there was a large gangland fight.

All in all, students assault staff and each other with great frequency and reckless abandon. People receive broken limbs and scarred faces. Weapons are confiscated. The article concludes, "The schools don't make the kids violent. The kids arrive violent."

My knee-jerk reaction to this piece is, "And?" I am not surprised. These are details of what most informed people know (but don't want to admit): School violence is a major problem facing today's public schools. However, this article and its details indicate for me far more disturbing trends: The divides in America.

The premier divide in this country is racial. Let's be honest: The majority of these schools and the participating students are African-American. So it comes as no surprise that the people who have been culturally disconnected and isolated from the mainstream have developed counter-culture behaviors that don't work with mainstream America. This is not too dissimilar to Native-American cultures, which some (mainly uninformed, middle-class Americans) deem them as having a "Reservation Mentality". I'm generalizing to make the point, but it seems as though, in the African-American community, violence being used to resolve conflicts seems more commonplace because there is a strong distrust of the police (and perhaps rightly so), and there are a number of community stigmas against appearing soft. The Italian and Irish communities of yesteryear also represented this type of vigilante village justice before they were absorbed into mainstream society.

Furthermore, we have the very real divide of the Bourgeois Black and the Ghetto Black. The former chides the latter for not being like them; go figure! Needless to say, the majority of these students are not in the first tier of the divide. I mean, let's be honest: A lot of African-Americans are pushed to the margins, and they don't mind staying there. It's similar to the statement, "Better the devil you know than the one you don't," which I suppose is why African-Americans are not afraid to continually perpetuate violence against each other regardless of the setting.

Another dominant divide in this country is economics. Again, it should come as no surprise that in a city deemed as one of the poorest in the country, these students reside on the side of town that is deemed the poorest within the city. This is a recipe for disaster, and the ingredients come together in the boiling pot of school. It seems to me that in urban America, there are many "No-Go" areas, of which some of these students are inhabitants. However, a school destroys the artificial barriers. It's similar to the way people go on a talk show to air their dirty laundry. Somehow, whether it's true or not, they feel that the talk show will act as a buffer when they do or say something they probably couldn't or wouldn't do at home.

Moreover, if you look at talk shows, I'm sure the guests predominantly represent the poorer people in our society, who don't seek out healthy ways to confront problems and don't have the money to hide behind. This speaks of the glass ceilings that exist within our society, and the ways people respond as a result of being kept at the bottom, whether real or imagined. As such, in poor or oppressed communities, respect and the perception of disrespect looms large. In these communities, a person can be killed for bumping into someone, for touching someone's shoes, for looking at someone funny, or even for being too effeminate if one is a male.

Another divide is that of parent-child relations. Continually, we send mixed messages to children — that they are innocent, they have rights, and they are the backbone of our society. All the while, we tell them to do what they want to do when they feel like doing it. Our boundary lines are blurred, so it is no surprise that these unsophisticated minds can't see properly.

Sadly, in one of the most startling nuances of the reporter's piece, a female student assaulted a teacher and stated, "My father is going to come up here and put a hole in you." This is indicative of a much larger trend: parental deflection. Parents, time and time again, are giving their kids a false sense of entitlement and bravado by coming to their aid even when they are dead wrong.

Instead of looking at their failures, parents pass on part of the upbringing of their children to teachers, yet they don't want their children disciplined by teachers.

Moreover, this divide fuels the 'I'll get you' mentality that seems to be so prevalent nowadays. If people aren't happy with a situation, they seek vengeance whether they are wrong or not. They sue, call the police, seek violent revenge, or call Child Protective Services or some other governmental agency to feel adequately redeemed.

In summation, I believe that this information needs to be shared with community and governmental agencies, parental groups, and students themselves, who are not likely to read the above piece or even know about this correlative information. This may help get to some of the root causes or at least stir debate that addresses this ongoing problem. But understand this first and foremost: The poor and disenfranchised are the main culprits of blue-collar crime, and the privileged are the main culprits of white-collar crimes. Perception is everything!

Iconoclast

As you have probably gathered by now, this whole book brings up double-edged terms. It does so because the worship of images or icons confronts all of us.

An iconoclast is one who seeks to overthrow traditional or popular ideas or institutions. The common figure that stands out most for me is James Dean. He was a '50s icon who showed many that navigating through life requires going through rough times in order to get to your desired destination, yet he was willing to be a rebel without a cause.

If you look at characters such as James Dean, they share a common trait: Charm. This is vital for us to grasp if we want a fuller understanding of the word 'charisma' (a personal attractiveness or interestingness that enables you to influence others). Remember the phrase, "He can charm your socks off."

That phrase alone, as tantalizing as it is, presents a dangerous person. It also speaks to how someone, whether male or female, has a certain way about them. They can through deviance or persuasion get their way. They aren't afraid to go against the grain to make a mark of their own.

So, although James Dean is not one of the true heroes of the modern age, he reflects the persona projected by many people nowadays. He personifies independence, cockiness, defiance, and, of course, rebellion.

I don't bring up James Dean to highlight his so-called baggage, because, after all, we all have baggage. Let's be honest; if you were to open up your baggage for us to look, what would be in it? Would there be promiscuity, drugs, gluttony, tattle-telling, hatefulness, racism, laziness, sexism, classism, et cetera.

The larger point I'm adamantly bringing up is that counter-culture is always in the mix. It is a driving force for us to seek to relate to one another in some form or fashion because we are endowed to do so. Yet, in doing so, we will attach ourselves to some iconic image. After all, I see many skateboarder types, hip-hop types, and so on; you catch my drift.

Hooked Up at Twelve

On a personal level, I was hooked by a young guy I thought was the greatest of them all. It occurred when I was twelve and full of myself. Like a lot of preteens, I was more than thoroughly convinced that this guy was the guy for me. It didn't bother me that others might like him; it bothered me more to be denied by him. He seemed to give me the self-esteem boost I apparently lacked. He was iconic to the point that he had me refusing to settle for less than what I thought I was worth.

I was so moved by him that I mentally erased my parents from the forefront of my mind and placed him in it. As I saw it, he was the love I needed, wanted, and was determined, even destined, to get, even if I had to lose myself in the process. Whatever it took, I was determined to get him no matter what the cost. I got him (as I will unfold), but it came at a serious cost.

Let me put it this way: He helped me to rebel with and without a cause. This was invaluable to me, because although my parents saw themselves as my gatekeepers, I saw them as troublemakers. In truth, I struggled with wanting to get back at or hurt others so that I didn't feel bad. That's why I got hooked on being hooked up.

The Body Rescue

This is a hard subject to talk about, but by the grace of God, let's deal with it. The thing is, when people are down in the dumps, especially financially, they use their body as a resource, a means to an end.

This will seem hardcore but, believe it or not, we are divided between selfish and social motives. It causes us to struggle to make ends meet. Even at the critical stage of our struggle, we have to transcend groups with selfish interests. Any person, including me, who tries to deal with the burning issue of 'using our bodies instead of our minds' needs to get a grip. By the grace of God, I can say that I've never had to rescue my body from being a resource. I have definitely known people who have, though, both male and female. I guess I was fighting so many other demons that it never appealed to me to outright use somebody in this way just because I could. Nevertheless, many people have the mindset of, *I'm going to use what I've got (my body) to get what I want (bills paid/other tangibles).*

The body issue is an ongoing power struggle that we all go through. This is why we must make healthy and wise decisions concerning our bodies, should stand firm on those decisions, and should not allow temptation to get the best of us in perilous times. We cannot undermine the struggle by thinking we cannot be conquered by temptation.

Again, this will seem disturbing, but in poorer communities all over the world, women prostitute themselves as a means to an end. More than that, it is a devilish treat that many savor. People fuss and fight over sex; it breaks up homes and hearts, and it's an overriding theme that we tend to fall for hook, line, and sinker. It's a Jezebel spirit that will make you think you are on top of the world. Now, bizarre as it will seem, sometimes, over your body, a man might cry, and over that same body, your spirit might die.

Put it another way, we all face physical, mental, and spiritual battles. No matter what stage of life you are in, your body is calling you to pay attention to it. It expects dividends to be paid to it. I learned that productive friendships make a world of difference. It's nothing like MTV and BET. Not being a slave to your body is empowering. This is a hard battle but worth fighting, especially if you learn to value the spirit-mind-body connection.

If it helps, meditate on the woman in the Bible who had an issue of blood. She wasn't a desperately-seeking Susan; she was a woman faithfully determined to have her body rescued.

Now let me share the misinterpretation of things.

Trickery

We constantly come up against people who like to play tricks. As I know that many of you have, I have met people who use trickery to get people to pay off their debts.

Their tendency toward thievery beckons them to become overly involved in their trickery. Some people unknowingly get caught up in other people's tricks, but they should at least suspect that they are being caught up in something. Figuring out what is that something is the million dollar question.

A thirteen-year-old girl, in order to show her mother that she could have a prettier baby than her eighteen-year-old sister, convinced or tricked an older guy in another town to get her pregnant.

How did she do it? She sexually teased a much older man, telling him that he could have her only after he taught her how to drive. Then she took her non-driving sister's birth certificate to the Department of Motor Vehicles and pretended to be the sister she despised. With the older man's tutoring, she passed her driving test on the first go-around.

She got rid of the old man by telling him that she would report him for rape if he didn't buy her a car. Begrudgingly, he purchased her a small, green AMC Gremlin. To keep up her charade, she parked the car three streets from her apartment complex.

Then, ready to accomplish her mission, she went to a town twenty-five miles away. When she got there and caroused in the streets, she found a man and could tell by the look in his eyes that she could knock him out by being a knock-out. She got want she wanted without him even knowing.

Her mother then not only had to deal with her daughter's pregnancy but with her dismal thought-pattern: This daughter was not going to be like the other one.

This story is a microcosm that reflects the deception and trickery that we are for and against depending on the circumstances. Count to three and say, "Oh, what tangled webs we weave when we first try to deceive." Let me add the word 'ourselves'.

Have you deceived yourself? Are you currently self-deceived? Trust me when I tell you that it's not all your fault. However, bear in mind that God's unconditional love and forgiveness is always hard for us to grasp. Too often we hope to escape the dangers rather than face the nitty-gritty truth about them. At times, our emotions not only put up warning signs, but they serve as a GPS system, informing us that we must run away from the apparent problem.

Still, how many times do we get duped? Upon reflection, I can say that my mother bestowed her best intentions on me. Yet I never received them as intentions; I caught them as shenanigans (tricky or questionable practices). It affected my behavior and sent me down a path of trying to get over by any means necessary — trickery, hustling, you name it.

Of course, this led to me acting out on many levels: With my boyfriend, in and out of school, or whatever else I could get into. I did so much during my teen years that people weren't afraid to point at me and proclaim, "That's the crazy one."

Narcissus

Whether it is misquoted or misunderstood, the term 'narcissist' is a very real and ever-present danger. For those of you who don't know, this term refers to a Greek mythological figure who fell in love with his own reflection. Nowadays, it refers to one who excessively admires himself or herself.

Let's be honest: This is a tough one. All of us fawn over ourselves at some point.

Like it or not, I have a dead reckoning with this term. I apply it to myself and my husband because we said 'I do' even when we did not. If that's confusing, try living through it.

You see, before we became brutally honest with ourselves, my husband and I were lost causes. I was into me, which means that I was addicted to him. He was into him, which means that he wasn't addicted to me, although he wanted me all to himself. That stated, our love was twisted and bizarre. Only a year and a half into our marriage, I felt like a stranger to my own husband.

The million dollar question is:

What is Love?

We can all be smitten and cursed by the same thing: Love. To be smitten is to be afflicted in certain degrees. To be cursed is to be harmed by someone or something. Both of these words imply emotions with one being essentially positive and the other negative.

Love is a bulldozer, hell-raiser, mugger, and gangster, but, at the same time, it is a rewarder, caregiver, enunciator, and more.

Depending on your circumstances, you may love or hate the concept of love. People respond to the word in different ways. Many take it as a deep-seated emotion and cherish it. They express it happily to someone in the hopes that the person can say it back. On the flipside, some are taken aback when someone says 'I love you' and they don't know how to respond.

Love has a variety of expressions. This is pivotal, especially in a world where people need a shoulder to lean on. Some people show love by sipping a cup of coffee to make sure it isn't too hot for their loved one. Some will travel thousands of miles to be with a loved one who has been in a near-fatal accident. At the same time, many parents will kiss their child's boo-boo. Sometimes, we tell our friends that we love them just to show our gratitude. So whether big or small, love is prescient, meaning it should guide your actions before they occur.

But love has dark sides. Love can also be mistaken for lust or infatuation, strong feelings that make us respond to situations.

Sometimes people feel unable to love; they cannot overcome lust. Even so, many believe that all is well while they serve both love and lust. I've heard someone ask, "If all is well, does it end badly?" The lady in question basically thought that her daughter's scandalous marriage was just good, clean fun. She was keeping quiet and letting her daughter sort out her wild ways.

Likewise, the lady pointed out that as a former "Deadhead" (an ardent follower of the band, The Grateful Dead), she loved partying and having fun. "Who cares if I left my daughter with other people as long as they fed her?" To her, it was all good clean fun as long as she wasn't a drag. She found out later that her daughter prided herself as being the child of a hippie-chick. She wasn't going to let virtue stop her from topping her mother, whom she saw as lame for settling down with a man in his late fifties.

Our early relationships influence our later relationships. The daughter used her mother's heyday as a working model of behavior. Even more so, she was determined to top her old lady. As a result, she became ruled by infatuation (possessed by an unreasonable passion or attraction) of a man she realized that she never really loved.

In the end, the lust to right her wrong put her in touch with a man whom she thought she could control. Sadly, when that so-called love went astray, her lust for life became a lust for death. Love, or the appearance thereof, reared its ugly head. She committed suicide rather than face the truth or overcome her depression.

I bring up that anecdote because many steps and missteps during the course of our lives have far-reaching consequences. Many of them have early-warning signs that many shrug off. I want you to take credit or criticism for your own responsibility in love.

In sharing with a friend about this book, she was compelled to remember an experience that occurred during her youth. As a young girl of 12, whenever she went to a nearby town, there were only two means of transportation she could use to get home: male neighbors who transported her by car for a small fee.

On one particular Saturday evening, one of the neighbors didn't take her straight home, but instead took her to a deserted area where he kissed her and told her how much he liked her. Being naive, she was flattered that an older male was attracted to her. This activity continued every time he had her alone in his car.

Then, one Saturday evening, he forced her down on the seat of his car and told her that he was going to "make her a woman". He weighed about two hundred pounds, so she couldn't even struggle.

When she finally got home, she was too scared to tell her maternal grandfather, because he would have killed the man. When she tried to tell her mother, she accused her of "messing around" with him.

Over the course of her life, she explained, she developed a deep-seated distrust of men. She had problems with male teachers and any men in authority. Finally, her ninth grade teacher told her that if she didn't get her head on straight, she was going to go crazy. Since this teacher was one of the few men she trusted, she tried to adjust her attitude.

Unfortunately, she admitted, the experience with the neighbor continues to cloud her thinking today. What bothers her most is that she has gone to church all her life. She had to finally acknowledge that going to church meant nothing if she didn't have the church in her. She is still struggling to learn to trust and love her fellow humans while living as God wants her to.

The definition of love that God uses best serves and protects me:

"Love is patient, love is kind. It does not envy, it does not boast, it is not proud. It is not rude, it is not self-seeking, it is not easily angered, it keeps no record of wrongs. Love does not delight in evil but rejoices with the truth. It always protects, always trusts, always hopes, always perseveres. Love never fails."

(Corinthians 13:4-5)

I steadfastly proclaim this version of love because it is the greatest of the three Christian graces: faith, hope and love. It is the one that goes beyond normal. It exemplifies self-examination to make sure that we are living up to a standard higher than ourselves. In that way, when we are not, we can humble ourselves.

Chapter Three

DESPERATE SEARCH

"Adversity is a test of character."

Anonymous

What's it all about?

In life there is a lot to learn. We cannot think that we know it all. We must be open to new lessons. We must even outgrow our old routines.

In my life, I have grown accustomed to seeing how plants impact people's nurturing. I live in a state that grows tobacco, which many crave. Besides that, I realize that there are many things that have helped me to grow myself to the point where I realized that selfishness is a hungry monster inside all of us.

I hate to burst people's bubbles, but I have to. First of all, we use the term 'real' much too loosely, especially in the Black community. Second of all, I think we fail to see or foresee that every stage of life involves a crisis at some point. It requires a constant reshuffling of how we view ourselves. It was clear to me growing up in the late '70s and early '80s that many forces were playing upon me. The invasion of the body snatchers was trying to get to my core.

During my teenage times, I felt so fragmented that I realized I had to put myself together. This led to me trying out different lifestyles or roles as if they were clothes. I was ready to find the niche that best suited me. I had no problem playing a church role in church. I had no problem playing a good student in school. I was so engrossed in role-playing that I would simply watch people on-screen and in real life to hone my act. I had no problem smoking cigarettes like a lady on Dynasty or from down the street. I had no problem drinking alcohol as long as it made me tipsy in some environments and self-assured in others.

Right off the bat, people thought I was a good girl. Perhaps I was, deep down; however, many saw the sides of me that I masqueraded to them. I was self-seeking beyond reproach. I had no problem being funny, cute, smart, silly, or whatever it took to get what I wanted. I was predictably unpredictable. I craved approval to feed my Frankenstein's monster. That part of me was trying to build itself up. It wanted to go from backstage to center stage.

At home, I did what I needed to get by. I was going through emotional ups and downs, and I loved and loathed the rollercoaster ride. Since my parents didn't model the behavior I wanted to incorporate, let alone adhere to, I simply played my part. My main goal was to achieve independence. My opinions were so different from my parents' that I had to go along just to get along. They saw me conforming to their standards, yet I could tell that they knew that my desire to assert myself was growing. I wanted to be large and in charge, and I did not want parental control ruling over me.

In another way, based upon the physical changes I was going through, I could tell that all of my fruits were becoming ripe. Along with my physical growth came moodiness; I was highly irritable at times, and my mouth was sharper than a razor blade.

Teenage Angst

It was clear to me, even as a teenager, that life is a struggle. It is clearer to me now that a large part of the struggle was self-interest. In other words, I was in my own way. Even though I went to church and may have thought I was living in Heaven, I was living in an emotional hell. Consequently, I could raise a million dollars' worth of hell if rubbed the wrong way. I had enough angst (anxiety, apprehension, or insecurity) to put on a mask.

The mask made me feel invisible and invincible at times. I would go to school and underachieve, even if I was smart enough to excel. Others knew that I was holding back, but I thought of myself as an independent person and that I could take care of myself. I didn't really need anyone else.

If I'd had it my way, I would have ruled the world with my boyfriend as the king and with myself as the queen. Deep down, there was something telling me that our relationship needed to have compromises and adjustments. Yet I dismissed that inner yearning because I wanted him wrapped around my finger. As soon as I compromised myself for him, he compromised my heart. Still, the more I wanted him, the more I saw that he wanted others, which made me want others to get even with him — a vicious cycle.

As I went through my turbulent teenage years, a deep uneasiness grew in me. I knew on some level that I was going through adversity similar to what the Duke and North Carolina basketball teams faced. I just could not connect the deeper meaning of adversity.

You need to understand that adversity is a test of character. Needless to say, I didn't grasp it. Instead, I developed defense mechanisms. I lashed out at and lied to people, especially my parents. I went round and round in disturbing cycles to show people that I was down for whatever.

Even before I got a license, I would take my parents' car for joyrides while they were gone. I would have friends stay over for the night and we would pretend to fall asleep. When my parents went to bed, I would break into my father's liquor cabinet and we would throw a private party. I acted as if I had forgotten what I had done and what I was going through. Some call that 'repression' or 'denial', but I was nonplussed (at a loss for what to say).

I am not alone in this self-serving endeavor. In the past, present, and future there are girls like me who have gone through the same things. As I will unveil, my own daughter, who was conceived during my self-destructive antics, is going through what I went through. I most certainly recognize myself in her.

Seeking Approval

I was struggling to find out who I was and what I wanted to be. I knew that my parents didn't understand what I was going through. My father thought I would work my way out of it. My mother saw it as a phase that I would simply outgrow. They thought that my behavior would even out.

40

I wanted to be accepted, which pressured me to try to fit in. I was constantly juggling the people I hung around with, what to do in my spare time, where to go, and when I could be myself at school and home. I'm sure you can relate to these types of worries. Interestingly, when I went into high school, my problems got worse. On one hand, I wanted to be the girl whom no one could deny, but on another hand, I was coming across many people who wanted to make me do what I didn't want to do. As I have stated before, I played roles involving sex, cigarettes, and alcohol.

My Boyfriend, Her Man

Let me share a regrettable tale of a friend of mine. I trusted her dearly and shared intimate details with her because I needed to bare my soul to someone. She was the person to whom I felt most comfortable telling my deepest, darkest secrets.

I shared sordid details with her that would make me blush today, especially about my relationship. I felt comfortable ridiculing his rotten ways, and I loved her laughter and jokes. I didn't feel threatened by her, even though she would sometimes unknowingly give me an inkling that she was interested in him. In the end, they slept together. This, of course, filled me with fire. I stewed and contemplated my retaliation. I was so torn and troubled that instead of simply crying 'foul', I decided to become vengeful.

I badmouthed them to whoever would listen and decided to up the ante by being with an outside party. As I seesawed back and forth over this pressing conflict, I felt as though I had found love on a two-way street but had lost it on a lonely highway. I find it ironic that intimacy is both a building block of a relationship and can bring you to your knees. Let this serve as a learning lesson. You can tell who's who by their appetite.

"Optimistic", one of my favorite songs, says, "As long as you keep your head to the sky, you can win." As an adult, those lyrics have transformed to me. Keeping my head to the sky means to stay in the face of God. As an adult, I've learned that I can't put my trust in human beings, since they'll let me down. I must put my trust in God; He won't let me down. It is written in Scripture: "I will look to the hills from which cometh my help, all my help cometh from the Lord."

As a teen, this was a crucial blow that ultimately made me stronger as an adult. I share this to inform young ladies that if someone has violated your trust, then placing yourself in unhealthy relationships and situations to try to get back at them will only cause you more harm.

That was a painful lesson to learn, but as a matured adult, I have successfully ended relationships when they were compromised, thereby limiting the offenders' ability to attain any new information to be used against me at a later date. Coupling the book with my own life has helped me to imagine the impact it has on the unsophisticated mind of adolescents and the toll it takes on them, because I was one of them.

I could go on and on about my escapades, but I'd rather you see an honest reflection in both yourself and others. Many teenagers have a variety of things going on in their lives that drive them crazy. To get approval, kids will make themselves available to a lot of wild and crazy ideas. Why do you think that the United States has a high teenage pregnancy rate? 750,000 teenagers get pregnant every year. Why? Approval!

There are a lot of girls who are confused about teenage pregnancy. In fact, 73% of teen pregnancies were not expected or planned. These pregnancies are caught up in the wave of approval-seeking. The decision to receive pleasure seems to override thoughts of consequences. Personally, if I had known that abstinence wasn't a felonious crime, I would have tried it. Instead, I sought approval from others even if it meant unprotected sex and the possibility of having a baby.

True to the Game

Look at your position. Your past, present, and future constantly intertwine.

During the preteen years, girls have more social intelligence and knowledge of how people relate to each other. Unlike boys, who are ready to make their fights physical, girls make their fights social. In other words, boys are more direct; girls are more indirect.

As you have gathered, I know this firsthand and secondhand. My daughter and I are eerily similar.

I struggled to relate with my parents. I still shriek when I think about how my father busted my lip because I didn't show him proper respect when talking to him. He showed me that he possessed a commanding presence. Although he didn't cheat on my mom *per se,* he showed me that a masculine love topples a feminine love. As ignorant as this might appear, I actually respected his side of love. It had more power and pizzazz. It contained the same superhero force as Popeye's spinach.

My mother's soft approach showed a lot of finesse but did not enforce power. Somehow, I realized that a balance of power is vital to life. After all, people vie and struggle for power. Some feel powerful while others feel powerless. I realized that the relationship between my parents had a stark power relation to it. At times, they were at odds with each other if she forgot who had the upper hand. Still, although their relationship had a fragile balance, my mother knew how to keep him off balance without him realizing it. She would use kind words, a nice meal, or a caressing touch. Between the two, they didn't realize that they were unwittingly instilling in me a teenage monster hungry for power.

I was so seduced by power that I decided to incorporate both of their styles into mine. My mother's style helped me to fit in as I deemed it necessary; my father's style allowed me to get back at somebody if I felt double crossed. I took 'Hell hath no fury like a woman scorned' and added a knockout punch, making myself a force to be reckoned with. Little did my father know it, but he gave me the power to act wild.

As trying as my teenage years were, I still saw it as a game. Realizing that games had ebbs and flows to them, I had no problem going through the dynamics of relationships as long as I asserted myself when the time was right. While this mindset presented challenges in school and relationships, I still felt like I was on top of my game.

As long as I could lean back on my parents and let them think they were running things, I was okay. As long as I was number one on my boyfriend's list, I felt adored. As long as I did okay in school, it didn't matter if I did good deeds. As long as I drank and smoked with the people who gave me a much-needed nod of approval, I felt like a Queen Bee. As long as I had "relations" with whomever I felt like relating with at the time, I was ecstatic. Whatever the game, I felt like a prime-time player.

I realized later that I understood why I had setbacks, and while that didn't make it easier to bear, I learned how to objectively compare myself to others in order to diffuse my ignorance and expand my worldview.

While going through the ups and downs of broken friendships and relationships, hurts, disappointments, rejections, betrayals, manipulations, and embarrassments, the years seemed to fly by. By the grace of God, I made it through high school.

My father emphatically stated that I had to either enlist in the military or attend college. Since I wouldn't dream of the going into the military, college became my reality, even though I didn't want to go. At Livingstone College, I was not highly enthused about succeeding, even though I knew I could.

Instead, I was captivated by having more freedom. I entered into my first two years of college with mostly the same mindset. I soon came to the realization that many of my fellow students thought the same exact way. As I look back, I realize that God sheltered me from many, many dangers, some of which I was too naïve to even notice.

I was unknowingly walking the path that God had laid out for me. I felt such a void that I needed something to cover it, and my then-boyfriend, now my husband, seemed like the perfect fit, as I'll tell in the next chapter.

Unrequited Love

Of course, love is one of the recurring themes in this book. It is one of the most mesmerizing words that we humans use. Now I would like to focus on unrequited love. This is when you love someone and they don't even notice. I attributed this to my then-boyfriend, now my husband, whom I met near the end of my sophomore year in college. My overriding concern was to become one with him.

It breaks my heart to reveal this, but I must: I loved him so deeply that I needed him to like me back, even if he was only pretending, and I was letting my mind play tricks on me. All I wanted was to stamp 'mine' on him. Yes, other girls could have him momentarily — but not for good.

Needless to say, this arrangement didn't last long. We broke up, and, as dysfunctional as it was, I missed him. Deep down I knew I deserved better, but I held out hope that the wrongs could be righted. Moreover, on the few occasions we ran into one another after we broke up, it was obvious that he missed me, too.

Thank God that just a few short months later, our relationship changed. We started to reconcile with a heartfelt belief that we were destined to be in each other's lives. We both decided to stop playing games with one another and have a 'real' relationship. We threw in the proviso that neither one of us would date outside the relationship. This would take effort, because we both were people who effortlessly attracted the opposite sex. We both were very charming, nice looking, and attention loving. At any rate, we both agreed to this committed relationship, and after we worked out all the kinks and glitches, it eventually worked.

Over the next year, we truly got to know each other more and more. In an ideal sense, we became very close as friends and lovers. This opened up the door to share our ups and downs, our dreams and disappointments, and even our past and current failures. Those eye-opening exchanges allowed us to bond. We stopped hanging out with others, and instead, in Romeo and Juliet fashion, we longed to spend every waking moment together. Family members on both sides felt that we were spending way too much time together, but we didn't let their opinions deter us from growing closer and closer.

As our relationship grew more intimate and serious over the next two years, we realized that we loved each other dearly. It could have been a breaking point, but, thankfully, it was a major *turning* point, because we realized that we were meant to be married with children. I got pregnant, and after the baby was born, responsibility surfaced and forced us to see the bigger picture and to see each other in different light.

It dawned on me that my husband was brought up in a broken home. His mother had him at a young age, but God's grace and favor allowed her to continue her education and obtain a four-year degree. Therefore, they were more like siblings than the more traditional mother-and-son relationship. His real father was not in the picture, and the man who replaced him was engaged in gambling, running numbers, boosting, drugs, liquor houses, and not being a wholesome father. By this time, there were two younger siblings in the picture. Although there were times when his stepfather taught him some things about manhood, his actions toward his mother stuck in my husband's memory. His mother had the same sort of unrequited love for his stepfather that I had for him. The after-effects of this love (domestic violence, drugs, alcohol) did not give my husband-to-be a shining example to follow.

By Hook or By Crook

A friend of mine shared a story with me that reflects the saying 'By hook or by crook' — that many of us will act wickedly and wildly to get over on people who we think are getting over on us.

The story involves a husband and wife who separated five times over a twenty-year span. Each separation involved him staying out into the wee hours of the night. When asked, he would rehash the same story: "All I was doing was hanging out with my boys." Of course, this would prompt the investigative reporter/ detective in her to ask probing questions of his boys. They, too, would dance around the truth as if they were in a Cirque De Soleil under-the-umbrella show. Therefore, she deemed them halfway crooks, with him in particular being a dirty scoundrel.

She threatening to call the police if he wouldn't leave. After her warm heart turned cold, she pretended to have nothing to do with him. Over time, she thawed out as he kept knocking down her defensive walls.

Quiet as it's kept, her husband is just like many of the men out there who fail to acknowledge their wrongdoing. They skirt around the truth by hiding behind a lie.

Women do the same thing. In this case, the wife routinely hooked up with an old flame when her fire needed rekindling. Yet as long as she hid behind her husband's wrongdoing, she could justify her own. As the saying goes, "Turnabout is fair play."

This cycle continued as they ignored the warning signs. They would go their separate ways only to return when the time seemed right. Uncannily, the rebound was invigorating to her on some level. She tried to pacify her husband by giving him what he deemed necessary for his approval: food, sex, and no backbiting. Before long, he would be contented, while she would be filled with discontent. Invariably, she would throw fuel onto the fire until their problems were rekindled.

At times, they wouldn't say a word to each other. He slept in the basement and she slept upstairs. After a heated quarrel, no reconciliation was in order, so one would leave instead of sitting down to talk.

The endless conflict reduced their marriage down to a smoldering fire but not a complete burnout. Why? They were overly defensive, which prevented honest communication.

Sometimes they wondered why they acted in such a way and if they each loved being the victim instead of the victimizer. In reality, they both justified their wrongs as doing right for the wrongs they perceived as being done to them.

The crucial moment of change occurred when the other man, whom the wife had been sleeping with, came to the husband and revealed the dark truth. Stunned, he went to her and finally admitted to his flings with prostitutes which were meant to boost his confidence. As heinous as she thought his acts were, she finally realized the detrimental aspects of her behavior and through squirreling and wiggling revealed her deep, dark secret to him. He was invigorated with rage, but it was quelled with the cold, hard truth of his own behavior. In the end, he was glad that they had cleared away a lot of confusion.

The number one question became, "Where do we go from here?"

The two got back together after realizing they were weaker when apart. Today, their steadfast determination to succeed is upheld by their mindful desire not to falter, especially by hook or by crook.

Ain't No Future

We were blessed with our daughter on July 26, 1993, an evening that I will never forget! My mother was there with me every step of the way. Everyone in his family and mine was elated. I was full of big dreams for the future of our little family. Still, first things first. I had about another year in school and he was working. My daughter and I lived with my parents while he lived with his mother. Eventually, my father let my then-fiancé move into one of his rental properties.

I spent some of my time at his new place and the rest at my parents' home with our baby. Interestingly, his current place was the same property in which my parents, albeit married, had lived with me as a baby. Therefore, my parents had adamantly made it part of their landlord arrangement that we could not 'shack up'. Our silent argument was that it wasn't such a big deal, since he and I were going to get married soon, anyway. Now that I think back on it, my parents had our best interests at heart, and they probably didn't want me to come to them six months later and announce that they would have another grandchild.

This gave my fiancé the best of both worlds; he could be a daddy and a fiancé at my mom's house and then be whatever he desired elsewhere, which usually meant chilling with his boys.

As time progressed, I felt that our relationship was worsening. My enthusiasm waned, and I felt trapped in marrying my child's father no matter what. I would look longingly at my boyfriend and feel obviously connected to him, but besides being the mother of his child, how deep was this connection? Yes, we loved each other. Yes, we had a child together. Yes, this is what we had planned—but something was missing. There was an old street term, "Ain't no future in your frontin'," which means that no matter what dreams you have, they're not going to come true.

His actions told me that he was immature and unready, but I thought that I was ready and that things would eventually work themselves out. This was a mirage, but I was determined to see it happen. The desire to be with him was tightening its grip on me. I already felt that I was just another statistic, and I was determined to fix that by making it right and not allow myself to be left holding the bag as were many other females I knew. I had always been the one who talked about women's lib and that I would never have a man's child and then desperately watch him walk away from us to go spread his love everywhere else. Occasionally, I would wonder if I was making something out of nothing. Perhaps he had that *je ne sais quoi,* an indefinable something that I simply had to have.

But wasn't *I* supposed to be that special someone?

The more I thought about it, the more I felt that I was in the exact same position in which I had always said I would never be placed. He and I had always talked intimately; one thing I had shared with him was that I never wanted to have children by different men and never get married to any of them. I had seen the struggles many of my friends and relatives had gone through when they really didn't deserve to be treated that way. They had to put their hopes and dreams on hold to raise children as single mothers with only the system to help, which was almost nothing. To survive, a struggling single mother could be driven to do things she had never had a desire to do.

When I decided to have his baby, I was determined to make him mine. I thought the baby would make him stay forever, and he had said we were going to get married. The more I thought this way, the more grateful I felt. At other times, though, I thought that I was thinking wishfully and that only time would tell.

My reason for bringing this up is to share with you a horrific disclaimer: We all need courage, but more than that, we need wisdom to guide it. I was young and unwise, so my courage was false.

Coming to terms with fears of my yesteryear allows me to show how it mirrors the faith I currently possess. I am more than a ball of unbridled emotions. I'm sure that you and others can see the same in yourselves. Being downtrodden or pushed around can make fear rear its ugly head. Trust me; there is no future in pretending to be something you are not. Even if you get away with it in the short term, you won't in the long term.

Hopelessly Dreaming

Everyone has hopes and dreams. Some dreams are bigger than others. Arguably, the high point of my life was realizing my life's objective: To empower others.

It's easy to dream, but hard to achieve. For instance, I was hooked on loving my husband before he actually became my husband. I didn't pay attention when people shook their heads disapprovingly. It should not befuddle anyone that I had my dream deferred, nor should it confound you that, despite the glaring warning signs that flashed continually, I was hopelessly devoted to him.

The warning signs and nay-sayings did not disturb my will to succeed. However, there were heated quarrels and cantankerous behavior across the board, although never any outright domestic violence. So, despite my determination, I knew something had to change immediately.

On the flipside, I had major second thoughts in the back of my mind, to the point that on my supposedly blessed day, I practically had an anxiety attack. I went to my parents' room, took off my wedding dress, and lay prostrate on my parents' bed. I felt a whole bevy of emotions, with fear being at the top of the list. My woman's intuition coupled with despair told me to give up. I lay on the bed sighing wistfully and crying. Disturbed by the thought of going through the day, I told my mother that it was a no-go.

My mother's life-coaching skills kicked into high gear, and she counseled me in an extraordinary way. She let me know that although I was experiencing a meltdown, I was simply second-guessing myself. She assured me that my ability to make it worthwhile was determined by me and my belief system. Steadied by her affirmations, I allowed my father to escort me down the aisle on July 29, 1995.

There was an initial wedding bliss, and we were happy on many levels. As the sands of time continued to dwindle, we came to the conclusion that what we had talked about early on in our relationship had come to pass. We had been together for four years, and much had occurred within that timeframe.

After our first year of marriage, my husband started to realize that commitment had a broad definition. For instance, there are major differences between 'married' and 'single'. For example, marriage is work; it involves a lot more give-and-take than he had previously realized. I think the foremost challenge was communication, because although we shared many years of communicating intimately with each other, there were more unanswered questions involved. What we realized was that there were many details which we had left out of our previous talks. Unfortunately, we had jumped all the way in and couldn't seem to reverse our course. I fully realized what it meant to feel unorthodox (not acting in a conventional way).

I was forced to change my mindset and realize that hopes and dreams are different for everyone. My hopes were restlessly tied to a man, which made me realize that even if you think you know a person completely, you may actually know little or nothing at all about them. Even if you've known someone for years, you might have only scratched the surface. At least — that was my experience.

I don't want to belabor this issue. I simply want to display the pitfalls of being out of sync with your mate. For example, there was a constant stream of arguing, some heavy and some light. We were tired of hearing and saying the same things over and over again and wanted to run each other out of our lives. To add insult to injury, we constantly accused each other of cheating.

Even though he was my husband and we were bonded together, I dismissed that as past tense. We had been inseparable in the past, but I could not see us rekindling that former affection. In fact, I could barely stand to see his face without some rip-roaring emotion swirling inside me. I would become inflamed and spew my disdain and contempt on him. I would always start on him about what a big disappointment he was to me. In return, he would dismiss me as a nagging nuisance and declare that my behavior was the major reason for his behavior, as if I was keeping him away.

Although he had given me a half-baked reason for his behavior, it made me think twice. I knew in my heart that the reason he was gone so much was due to his need for attention and to be center stage. No wonder he was running game everywhere. He was used to women letting him be the center of attention; who was I to break that trend?

I got tired of stroking his ego when it ceased to pacify him to the point of treating me like a good wife. I could no longer allow him to come and go as he pleased. At times I felt like the editor in chief of some big-time newspaper, the way people were reporting the news about my husband to me. It also didn't help matters that the city we lived in was very small. We all know how news travels fast and how hard it is to keep secrets, especially in a bite-sized city where everyone knows everyone. I soon came to realize that what's done in the dark shall come to the light, and what's said in secret shall be shouted from the rooftops.

Upon fully realizing that marriage is a very serious thing, I started to go through a season of depression, and it took a lot out of me. I no longer felt lucky to be married. I could no longer envision myself as a contestant on some wonderful reality show. My marriage was not only failing, but it was taking a major toll on our mental and emotional health. We couldn't provide for my daughter like we wanted to. I had a degree but had only been on starter jobs. My husband was always gallivanting with strangers and his friends. We had no real income. Things had gotten out of hand.

I strive to introduce you to the serious reality of marriage because it is ideally portrayed as Heaven on Earth, which can propel you to get married early on. However, hopeless dreaming can force you to evade reality.

For example, our marriage was not helped by our environment. We lived in one of the most drug-soaked and crime-infested areas in our city. That made me remember what I once heard a wise man say: "Love is blind and marriage is the eye-opener."

Feeling dazed and confused, I kept wishfully thinking that our marriage would work itself out. Part of what spurred me was that I had been miraculously cured of a heart murmur despite my smoking habit, which made me rethink my strategy. Something told me that my husband and I could become one; I transferred that intuition into hope and dreams despite constant evidence to the contrary.

I began to realize that life is full of ups and downs. On the ups, we would be as madly in love as when we first met. During the downs, which were usually prompted by my silent treatment or spurts of anger, he would fight back with sordid behavior, and we would treat each other like total strangers. The more I realized how ultimately destructive our relationship was, the more I realized that our marriage had seen its best days and that the end was knocking on the door.

Sick and Tired

One of the things that came to mind when I realized that my life held more in store than what we could actually carry is that I had gotten sick and tired of it. I was fed up on so many levels. On that note, I realized that my continual hurts were plaguing me mentally, physically, emotionally, and spiritually. I realized that I was addicted to him, yet in grand irony, he wasn't that addictive. In that respect, I realized that there was indeed a thin line between love and hate, especially when he was taking my love and his lust toward others without any regard to the hate he was conjuring up in me.

Eventually, a straw broke the camel's back. I had accused my husband of visiting a certain young lady; she then indirectly sent me a message about what she would do to me if I approached her about my accusations. I went directly to her front door, but, fortunately, she was not home or would not come to the door.

After I had cooled down, I sent her a nasty message. She came to my front door accompanied by family members. One of them began the opening statements for her, I stood on my front porch, amazed by what was happening. Many different thoughts were racing through my mind, one being that this was the first and would be the last time I would deal with drama like this.

When I realized that he was somebody else's man and that I was only married to him and living with him, I decided to let the marriage go. After just a year and a half of marriage, it was over, and my feeling was, *Good riddance.*

At times, we are so enthralled by our emotions that we don't see how they affect our minds. We must not simply react; we must think as well. If there are issues plaguing your mind, I challenge you to fully contemplate them. I also encourage you to search your memory and pull out a reflective anecdote. It will give you a fuller view of life.

So much of my world was a created illusion, but it had to collapse right in front of me in order to make me see the truth. My misadventures and rude awakening disillusioned me. Afterward, so much went missing in my life that I wondered if I could overcome such a drastic change.

Empowered by that awakening now, I prayerfully regret not having full cognition of it at the time. Does the same hold true for you when things fall apart on you?

Obtain and/or Achieve

Choosing between obtaining and achieving can be as difficult as solving a Rubik's Cube. There is always an inclination to cheat, whether by asking someone to teach you all the right moves and then letting them solve it, by buying a new one and proclaiming it as an old one, or by switching the stickers around. Yet, when push came to shove and someone asked you to do it again, your words failed ("Um, well, you see, uh...").

Life is a process and involves tradeoffs, twists, turns, maneuvering, contemplation, frustration, and more. I understand the challenges that many of you face. I share my life's journey with you to reveal the thin lines between counter-forces. For instance, I know there is a thin line between love and hate, because I have walked it as if I was in a circus. Likewise, I also know that there is a thin line between the birth and death dates on a tombstone: such as, 1920–2000.

I'm a big believer in balance. I think that life should be a good balance of everything. Still, I am wise enough to know that we all get off-balance when we don't know how to adjust ourselves.

I'm sure some of you remember how much Mary Lou Retton captivated us when she did her wonderful gymnastics at the 1984 Olympics. She obtained an overall high score in all-around gymnastics and won a gold medal. How many of you can jump rhythmically on a balance beam?

It should be liberating and exciting to all of us to know that many opportunities for growth exist when we are forced to choose. The choices will be hard, but even if they bring forth regrettable decisions, they are well worth it.

Chapter Four

GROWING PAINS

"Commitment is the cognitive component of love."

Anonymous

Trust

According to the dictionary, trust is 'reliance on the character or truth of someone'. Inevitably, trust plays a huge part in our lives. Would television or movies work without it? I don't know why this vital element is so elusive to us; it is woven into the fabric of human lives.

I firmly believe that gaining someone's trust is a key ingredient to the betterment of a good relationship. We cannot miss a larger point than trust. It involves truth and untruth. Have you ever heard the phrase, 'Trust nothing after dark'?

Interestingly, trust is coupled with rapport, which is established with viable connections to people, situations, and things.

The Life and Times of Me and You

If we are honest, then we are beckoned to search for and reach higher heights. We are commissioned to become 'good' no matter what that really means. Human history is riddled with the same 'goodness' we are meant to bestow. It's as if there is an unknown realization that all of United Souls have good and bad stirrings within us.

The novel, *The Giver,* portrays 'sameness' as Heaven on Earth. In it, everyone is the same; no agonizing pain can affect them. As in *The Communist Manifesto*, the government enforced strict rules and regulations. Sameness spread like an epidemic flu as people ate the same meal at the same time and dressed the same.

The novel alleged that if there is no choice, all sin or evil sanctions are removed. No one can hurt themselves or others, especially if their point of view is taken away or made the same as that of others.

But if we are honest, life is about variety. Whether good or bad, people are individuals and vary in numerous ways. Food and water are common human needs.

In our lives, we are tantalized to assert our individuality, such as through styles and clothes. The chain reaction can be seen all over. People are more interested in asserting their individuality within a clique than they are while solitary. As such, things are more intertwined than most people realize.

People are more likely to recognize a picture of Michael Jackson than Franklin D. Roosevelt. This is due to us being far more selective than we care to admit. We select entertainers, lifestyles, insignias, sports teams, and more, to convey a trait at the desired time. In this way, we are all both the same and different, whereas we select what both suits us individually and makes us fit into the collective.

I know this firsthand. As a North Carolinian, I'm expected to love a North Carolina team in college sports. Inside North Carolina, the battle lines are redrawn based upon proximity. Only when it comes to the Olympics can I root for all of America. We are constantly making changes and choices that we then have to live with.

I had very mixed emotions when I took my daughter, left my husband, and moved back in with my parents. I was mentally and emotionally drained and broken, yet I still allowing pride to take the wheel. Resentment and bitterness broiled inside me. I was determined to show him that he was not irreplaceable. I was determined to make him feel the same hurt that I had. I made up my mind that 'homeboy' was going to pay.

During our separation, I did many vengeful, hurtful, spiteful, and just plain evil things to him in order to discredit him as a man and as a husband. I could feel myself spinning out of control despite a still small 'something' that I often felt tugging at me. At the time, my parents would often urge me to take things slow and seek God for help. I was feeling convicted, yet I chose to ignore the innermost parts of me that were screaming, *I GIVE UP!*

I knew his hang-outs and associates, and I made mine as far in the opposite direction as possible to avoid any public scenes, since I conducted myself less than civilly anytime we communicated. He was doing his thing, but according to reports, his game needed a little work. But so did mine; I was just going through the motions with no real intent or purpose.

We both went nowhere fast in our endeavors to make each other look bad. So much had occurred in such a short amount of time that we ran out of steam. It was time for some serious intervention. Little did either one of us know that it would come from above.

Out of the blue, my husband called me and told me that we needed to talk. For some strange reason, I let my guard down. We got together and talked about everything that had occurred. He expressed his remorse about our separation, his infidelity in our marriage, and how he intended to do whatever it took to make things right between us. He wanted me to know that he was ready to be faithful and committed. Ultimately, he expressed his need to have his family back.

Being together forever with someone seems so wonderful but yet impossible. Is it?

I was confused and had mixed emotions. One of my concerns was that even if we eventually reconciled, it would never be the same. We all have a bad habit of being unyielding while disdainfully accusing others of being unyielding.

Thankfully, something inside me was telling me that I couldn't help him until he was willing to help himself. I knew that growth was inevitable.

Please bear in mind that wherever you are in your life, your growth will not end until it is complete. I hope that gives you a glimmer of hope. You might feel sick and tired, but press on. If it doesn't kill you, it only makes you stronger!

After all had been said and done, he was looking into my eyes and I into his. I was so torn. I just wanted to know how to ease my pain.

I eventually decided to charge it to the game (to consider it a lesson learned). During our separation, I had realized that we both had played a high-stakes game with our marriage. I expressed a whole array of emotions and sought approval. In a bizarre twist of fate, when he made me feel dejected and rejected, I transferred those feelings right back to him.

We both made bad choices. I chose to give up my affection for him in exchange for a friendship with the world. In the end, that changed us both.

Interestingly, this fiasco made us both think of our love on another level. We realized that this love encompassed intimacy, passion, and commitment. Intimacy grows steadily in the early phases of a relationship but later tends to level off. Passion develops quickly and then typically levels off, motivating the relationship, and involves a high degree of physiological arousal and an intense desire to be united. Commitment is cognitive; it increases gradually at first but grows more rapidly as a relationship develops and matures.

At that point, our commitment was definitely where we desired it to be. I realized that his love was all that I wanted, provided that I could learn to ignore my bad feelings and relate to him in a way that would make our relationship a long and enduring one.

Thankfully, I realized that in exchange for giving up my new, erratic lifestyle, I would get my family back. I chose my family, and although putting our marriage back together was risky, it was worth it.

We agreed that we needed each other to survive. This time it would be all or nothing. We both realized that God was the reason for our reconciliation and that we needed to get closer to Him. We also realized that there was lots of work to do and lots of changes to be made on both ends.

Relatable

My husband and I began repairing our marriage with the help of God's supernatural intervention. He brought restoration to our relationship, but we had to first surrender everything to Him.

I also started to shed light on my relationship with my daughter, since she was a carbon copy of me in many ways and the main reason why I eventually delved into the nature of relationships.

I wonder if the definition of the word 'relationship' is either changing or being completely lost. People seem to use it so loosely these days. I believe the computer and all this instant messaging is cheapening the word.

Relationships have always been an integral part of human existence. Great lengths were gone to in order to keep them intact. In the past, before computers and telephones, sending letters could keep a relationship alive. Receiving one was a much-anticipated and cherished event; there was something special, reassuring, and binding about seeing a loved one's handwriting.

Nowadays, I receive loads of emails from people I don't even know. They address me by my first name as if we were friends or in a relationship. They want to get me to buy this or sign up for that. I don't like it. I resent the time I have to spend clearing their junk out of my inbox. Moreover, I can't help but think of all the children and adults who are lured into 'relationships' over the Internet. Do we really even know what a relationship is?

Nexus Point

In her book, *Odd Girl Out,* Rachel Simmons shares the story of a bully named Deirdre who shows off to her friends by mistreating a girl named Elizabeth. To quote the book, "She pointed and laughed from the lunch table and insulted Elizabeth at recess, often using what she knew intimately of Elizabeth to sharpen her barbs."

It is untrue that women are always perfect nurturers and caregivers. Women are prone to silent violence that is as debilitating as outward violence. We like things to go our way, and when they don't, our silent violence becomes silent treatment. Ask men; they are constantly battered with ill-respect, namely, silent treatment.

In stark contrast, when females deal with other females, it can get fierce beyond belief. The movie, *Mean Girls* portrayed this reality. Girls spread rumors, shun others, and seek the in-crowd as if afraid that they will go out of style. When seeking vengeance, while guys are more likely to use brute force, girls are more likely to backbite and backstab.

We have to deal with this honestly. The central point that we must come to terms with is that of integrity. I heard someone say, "Real integrity is doing the right thing, even if nobody finds out." Having integrity is hard to achieve, yet it is relevant and beneficial, because, inversely, low integrity allows us to become "Mean Girl" or "Queen Girl" and leave a lot of destruction in our wake.

The subject of integrity is very near and dear to my heart, because of all the heartache I experienced due to the lack of it in our relationship. God constantly reminds me of the Bible story of Joseph running from Potiphar's wife as she attempted to seduce him in private. He chose not to sin against God with his body or violate the trust his commanding official had for him.

What things have you done when no one was looking?

High integrity lends peace of mind and leaves you satisfied about having done the right thing. Inversely, having no integrity causes you to lose the respect and trust of others, to lead a troublesome life, and to endure guilt and insecurity.

Odd Girl III

In *Odd Girl Out,* a Hispanic woman from Arizona said of African-American girls, "The heart of their resistance appears to be an ease with truth-telling, a willingness to know and voice their negative emotions." (p. 178)

It has been my experience that in the African-American culture, you are expected to 'tell and be told' (to provide and expect openness about emotions). Upon reflection of my article about violence in Atlanta public high schools, I realized that even though it may be more accepted to voice feelings, the outcome is only more violent if the emotion being shared is aggression.

Without the violence, I can see the positive side of expecting to tell and be told. I wish everyone could be like that. But then again, I had better be careful of what I wish for; I don't know if I feel like being 'told about myself' today.

I understand the reason why they seem to be passionate and forceful. The question that keeps popping into my mind is, *If they dish it out, can they take it?*

So Unique

I will share with you two pivotal stories that will help us understand each other and foster mutually-beneficial relationships.

Although I changed the name of this first girl 'to protect the innocent', this story is about anything but innocence. It involves a seven-year-old Baltimore girl named Donna. She had very common problems and shows the intergenerational dynamics that we all must go through in one way or another.

She was being raised by her grandparents because her parents were in prison. She was well-behaved, topnotch in school, and courteous to a fault. Her grandparents were active in her life, taking her to museums so that she might be influenced by a wide variety of cultures.

Donna's mother had been raised very similarly, except that her parents had thought that she would grow out of her teenage, boy-crazy phase. Instead, she not only masked her pain and deceit, but she also tried to outdo her husband in crimes and drugs. She was not so unique.

Not So, Madam

Culture is ever-present in our lives in some variety or another. I bring that up to share a cultural hero from African-American history. Her name was Madam C. J. Walker. She was the first Black female millionaire, because she built a hair care empire by developing hair care products.

Look at Essence Magazine and you will see her influence on models. Although she died in 1919, she was a hallmark with an ironclad faith in God and herself. However, as heroic as she was, the prime focus of this piece is her daughter, A'Lelia Walker, as written about by her great-great-granddaughter, A'Lelia Bundles:

"As many parent/child relationships are, theirs was very complicated. Madam Walker rose up from abject poverty, founded her own business, and eventually became one of the most famous people in the country. As a mother, she intentionally spoiled her daughter but also wanted her to be successful. As a result, A'Lelia Walker became a very complicated person. It is pretty simplistic to say, as some do, that Madam Walker made the money and A'Lelia Walker squandered it. In actuality, A'Lelia had a lot of great ideas, but only one person could lead, and she often felt overshadowed or dismissed by her mother. It was very difficult for her to live up to her mother's expectations, which is probably the case for fifty percent of the population, it is just that the rest of us are not as famous."

I bring up this piece to show the importance of spreading our love so that the bounty will be widespread. I'm not trying to cause you anxiety but to get you to acknowledge that generational changes and cultural shifts are as common to us as food and water. Did people drive cars in 1850? Was television important to Christopher Columbus? Is Barack Obama the first man to be president? Have we had a woman president yet? Are the Flintstones a topflight cartoon?

Chapter Five

INFLUENTIAL CHOICES

"And just as you want men to do to you, you also do to them likewise."

Jesus, Luke 6:31

At this stage in my life, I triumphantly realize that my hard times have given me a deeper understanding of my life choices, good or bad.

I remember thinking about cavorting with my husband. He had made such an impression on me that I was awestruck. Although my decision to get with him was not an easy one, it was hard for me to say "No" when my body was saying "Yes".

At that time, I was inclined to go with what I felt. I was comfortable with being guided by my emotions and going with the flow. Even though it was my own decision, my opinion was influenced by a variety of people.

This goes against the beacon of trust, but personal agenda can deeply influence our lives. That is why I constantly reiterate the value of the choices we make, since we are forced to live with them whether good or bad. I share my life with you so you can compare it to yours and with the lives of others.

In this particular chapter, let me show you how my life choices intertwine with choices of others. Bear in mind that although guilt doesn't always show on our faces, it all too often shows up in our life choices.

A Hard-Knock Life for Us

We live in an imperfect world of shifting boundary lines on race, gender, and economics. Let us not forget our past.

This point is embodied by Margaret in the book, *The Keepers of the House* by Shirley Ann Grau. She grew up to realize that she was starkly different from others. Her dark skin showed her mixed heritage of Black, White, and Native American. Everyone around her was White. Her past reflected her present while threatening her future. To make matters worse, she was judged by whether or not her actions reflected the negative stereotypes others projected onto her.

She realized that her jailer was not free; therefore, she suppressed her anger and resentment. In fact, she understood that although she was dark on the outside, her inside was White.

Furthermore, as she went into adulthood, she was still tarnished by her past. Finally, she started to let the mistreatment turn into fuel for fire. She blazed away her false perception of self in order to finally realize that she was a maligned figure and that change had to come from within. That allowed her to overcome her obstacles and achieve much higher standards. Her lesson serves as a valuable lesson for us all: Our pasts are not the road map to our future, even when they force us to detour.

I share that story to show that your hard knock may be different than mine. Let's admit that Mr. or Mrs. Jailer may have some right to hold you back. How you internalize your perception of their action will externalize your reaction.

The Forgotten Rule

The Golden Rule is 'Do unto others as you would have them do unto you.' But in our selfish 21st Century, is this standard even applicable?

This is a universal concept, yet when self-preservation, self-aggrandizement, self-fulfillment, and self-actualization is promoted more than McDonald's, is the Golden Rule just tarnished spray paint? Selfishness is a powerful mindset and a hallmark of our survival story, while applying the Golden Rule and living to serve others threatens one's self-preoccupation.

You should always value yourself, but the 'Looking Out for Number One' frame of mind is an unhealthy extreme. Finding the right balance is a challenge that besets us all. It helps, as I was forced to learn, for us to understand benevolence (the disposition to do good and the desire to promote the happiness of others).

Upon realizing my own self-absorption, I recognized how, in modern times, benevolence is difficult and pales in comparison to selfishness. People care for themselves over others. We'd rather close ourselves off in isolation or join a crew, clique, or gang than exercise the Golden Rule.

I'll admit that applying the Golden Rule requires a deep soul-search. It requires that you put others first, which seems unrealistic to us, as we are constantly bombarded with self-promotion. We conjure up the evil done to us by others and ignore the good.

A friend shared a very classic example involving a woman who received a $3,400 tax return. She asked her father to drive her and her children all over town to spend the money. They spent all day from 9.30 A.M. to 7.20 P.M. buying things for her and her kids, but not a meal for her father, let alone any gas for the ride.

When the car's tank was empty, she chastised her father for not having enough gas to take her and her kids back home. When they finally made it home, she went into the house cussing and fussing, hoping to get the rest of the family on her side. Her wish was granted, filling her with false pride.

No one spoke a word in her father's defense except her youngest son, who asked, "How come we go to church all the time but don't practice what they preach?" He was ignored by the adults.

In a world where our hearts get broken and our will gets distorted, maybe the Golden Rule is not as good as the golden crispy nuggets. What's your take on it?

Desperate People Do Desperate Things

As I was progressing through my life's changes, it struck me that people do the darnedest things. Looking for their reasoning was like searching for a needle in a haystack until I realized that we sometimes operate out of fear, especially when we come in contact with people who are tough to please.

I'm amazed when I hear stories about why people did this or that to overcome some malady, and I'll share a story to drive this point home.

There was a woman diagnosed with bipolar disorder, which caused her to have many different moods and personalities. She had manic highs and raved like a lunatic; she had depressed lows and slept more than Rip Van Winkle. Her life was unbearable.

During the '90s, she shunned her Costa Rican Black heritage and religion to become a Jehovah's Witness. She thought her new group had all the answers, yet she went from Kingdom Hall to Kingdom Hall, trying to find the right one. She even went to a predominately Spanish-speaking Kingdom Hall, even though she hated being a Latina and light-skinned Black woman.

During the new millennium, she saw a growing disdain for Hispanics that matched hers. To separate herself further from her heritage, she changed her name. All of a sudden, she became an African-American and was angry because she had never classified herself as such. She retreated even further, as if she could never be integrated into society.

In truth, her parents are from Costa Rica. How did she lose her heritage? Sometimes, when we are being pretentious, we need to be told, "Don't even stress that." It might sound rude and crude, and we might miss the kernel of truth within. Someone who confronts us with this truth isn't just sneering at our charade; they are trying to help us help ourselves. Even if they don't know how to address our problem, they aren't our enemy for trying. Give credit where credit is due.

We shouldn't desperately search for a way out when the answer may lie within.

Able Responses

We often lose sight of the fact that privileges, responsibilities, and rights are often linked together and are sewn into the fabric of our lives.

Typically, people are responsible for achieving or maintaining a favorable result. It is implied that the person will make a conscientious effort to do what is expected of them. The end result doesn't always justify the means. I'm sure that right now you could think of ten examples within ten minutes.

What is Responsibility?

"Our greatest tragedy is not death, but failure to accept responsibility."

Ronnie Nsubuga

People sometimes pretend to know what they need to do, and their plans sound pretty good. However, irresponsibility is woven into the fabric of our lives, especially when we want to assert our independence.

Doing the right thing because it is expected does not make you 'good'. There are sins of commission and omission. It's not just what you do but what you don't do. Of course, being responsible has an upside, but don't use it as an excuse to lord yourself over others.

There is a downside to shirking responsibility. I have watched home-cleaning shows on which people justify living in filth. It's not that they can't clean up; they just don't want to be bothered. They'd rather walk around in their mess then clean it up. They don't respond to their situation.

One of the kids on the show preferred killing people in video games over killing the mess in his room that was growing large enough to smother him. The thought of living responsibly made him shake his head.

We all need to clean up our acts. It's a lot easier to shirk responsibility than to overburden yourself with it. Either way, it puts up and takes down many barriers in our lives. Our ability to respond is worth paying a price to understand.

Sabotage

Peace is 1% inspiration, 99% hard work and compromise.

Relationships are often sabotaged in one way or another, and you and I might actually be guilty of it.

Expressing goodwill to people who have harmed you is a diabolical challenge. We are stunned when this reality takes precedence in our lives.

I once heard of a woman living in Middle-America who was forced to deal with the aftermath of abusive relationships. She was born the oldest girl of ten kids, and growing up in the '70s and '80s, she was so jealous of her three older rough and tumble brothers that she constantly tried to emulate them. Furthermore, she didn't like the fact that she had a Muslim name, especially when she went to a Christian church.

She wanted to be as attractive as Jayne Kennedy but looked nothing like her. Beset with that fixation, she became a laughingstock. Boys ran away when they saw her coming. To show them, she turned to chasing girls the same way she expected to be chased. She had many takers, especially those who were desperate for attention and loved all the lies she told them.

She even convinced three of her four sisters to act the same way. To add insult to injury, she convinced at least seven of her nieces that hers was the dominant and preferred lifestyle. The diabolical liaisons reflected an ugly truth: A lot of domestic abuse occurs between these women. The common perception is from man to woman, but let's get wise.

She still professes a desire for men, but as soon as she thinks of light-skinned women, she suddenly hates men to the point of wishing they would all die. She is a stern example of self-sabotage.

She is quick to say, "I want you to suffer like I did," because she doesn't want people to live without her. She loves to leave an indelible impression. However, she doesn't want to be *persona non grata* (unwelcome), so she constantly tries to make herself seen, felt, or heard.

She is reminiscent of many. Do you know someone like her?

Ramifications

A contributor to this book shared a teaching tool that they use while trying to help their students understand the ramifications of their actions. It reflects a lot of us at some stage in our life.

Causes of Suicide: Drugs, alcohol, depression, stress, past experiences, race and/or religion.

Effects of Suicide: Death, suffering of family and friends.

Prevention: Visiting counselors, friends and peers, teachers, and family, staying away from drugs and alcohol.

Causes of Drugs and Alcohol Abuse: Peer pressure, stress, depression, parental influences.

Effects: Death, addiction, failed relationships, failure in school, ruined life, health problems (liver disease, colon cancer, heart damage and disease, neurological disease).

Prevention: Seek help, avoid tempting situations, respect yourself.

Causes of Anorexia Nervosa and Anorexia Bulimia:

Feelings of being overwhelmed and powerless, low self-esteem, poor body image, peer pressure, relationship problems, anxiety, personal history.

Effects: Depression, health problems, mood swings, hair loss, lack of concentration, anemia, low blood pressure, heart and kidney failure, dehydration, fatigue, pregnancy complications, weak bones and muscles, growth problems, and isolation from family and friends.

Prevention: Get help, eat healthy, maintain a healthy body image.

In that breakdown, I see relationships — family and friends — interwoven throughout. This teaching tool informs us how vital it is to choose healthy, positive, safe, and therapeutic relationships. It is important to build close bonds with family and friends and to find at least one person with whom you can feel comfortable sharing your innermost thoughts and desires.

It also teaches that you must learn to say no and mean it. Don't be easily influenced, especially by negative forces. Respect yourself and your body.

A Means to an End

Too often people speak about the outcome as though nothing led up to it, as though the result just appeared out of thin air. It becomes a marketing statement: "Just do it." Do what?

Don't treat people as objects or a means to an end. This way of thinking is so ingrained in us that we don't know a world without it.

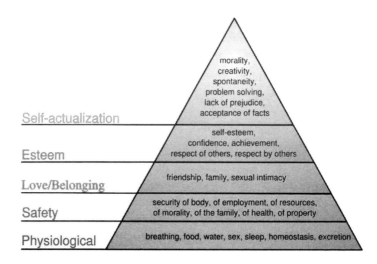

Additionally, I raise Maslow's hierarchy of needs, which illustrates that progress is achieved level by level.

That is the essence of the spirit as it relates to the mind and body. To some, it's simply an element of the mind.

THE GAME OF LIFE

"He that plants trees loves others besides himself."

Thomas Fuller

We have all heard it said that life is like a game. Most games, whether played alone or as part of a team, have well-defined rules with clear benefits for winning and costs for losing.

Life is full of interactions. We are constantly competing and collaborating as individuals, groups, and nations. Your life consists of games in which you have to make decisions factoring in one or more people. Game theory concludes that any situation with two or more people that requires decision-making can be classified as a game.

Playing games is something that comes naturally to humans. Perhaps the most interesting thing that human beings do is compete and collaborate. How we do with almost any strategy depends on the actions of others and our responses to those actions.

We easily understand the rules, and by playing against more experienced players, we pick up the subtleties and overcome difficulties of a particular game.

In some games you will know everything, while in other games you will have to guess. Sometimes competitors work together to survive; sometimes cooperation is impossible, since the winner takes all.

Point of View

We tend to interpret the world based on our worldview and our own reality. We all have a lens through which we view the world. We must understand point of view. This is a multi-layered adjustment, as I was coming to understand. You need to be balanced in order to adjust to a given situation.

As I reunited with my husband to rekindle our family, I had an uncharacteristic shift of point of view and saw how much it impacts all of us. We all go through many life-altering events. Understanding how others make adjustments helped me learn how to recognize when to make my own adjustments.

Little Things, Major Focus

Here's an anecdotal occurrence that reflects the impact of perspective:

In 2006, Ivory Latta, a North Carolina basketball superstar, led her team to victory against the Tennessee Volunteers and advanced to the NCAA Final Four. Although Latta was evenly matched with the Volunteers' star, Candace Parker, she showed a tenacity that outmatched her opponent. Down the final stretch, Latta made six free throws and sealed the victory.

Likewise, every time the Volunteers came at them, Latta and her teammates met them emphatically and refused to quit. As emotionally debilitating as life can seem, there is a fountain of hope inside each of us, where we can refresh ourselves.

Let's Stay Together

Staying together is easier said than done. We tend to rationalize our behavior through self-deception.

I will share two letters sent by a husband to his wife who had forced him to leave because of religion. They both were Christians, but they could not come to an agreement on how they would serve God. This first letter was in response to her extending an olive branch:

> "Thanks for the reply; it helps heal the fractures. Nonetheless, I realized a long time ago that you lacked the courage to really move closer to me, and every time you did, you got scared. Likewise, I realize that my actions gave you the corroborating evidence to justify your actions or inactions. Therefore, I knew that I must love you enough to let you go if I saw that you lacked the courage needed to move closer to me.
>
> Last summer, despite wanting to move closer to me, you lacked the courage. That pushed me away for good. Again, you had my actions to justify you and a bully named Ann to enforce your decision. For that reason, I pray that the next man will keep the criteria checklist full of the pros while he's under severe scrutiny.

Moreover, our son stood to suffer from one-sidedness and heavy-handedness. The thing is, if Brian and I are ever to have a true bond not undermined by your negative perception of me, I need to move away from that position you take when you feel you're not getting your way or are unhappy with my behavior. That is the part that undermines me, sells me short, and that Brian often complained about.

I'm not trying to fight with you; I'm trying to create peace. However, I must be adamant that you come out of your comfort zone to do so. There is no sense in a person like me upholding Christian values to a person who is supposed to be more Christian than me, even if I now know that your values are more nominal than I had realized. In that case, I could just be like you and act as though I have no responsibility to God, especially to others who think and act like me. If that makes me cold and self-righteous, why is that different than anybody else?

I have to live from the core of my being. That essay is reflective of who I was before I met you. This is the person I simply must be, despite who you think I am. It's funny how hard times can turn a person's life around. It bothers me how much you have never maintained the heights that your father preached.

As times goes by, my goal is to draw closer to Brian because I know that once he turns into a teenager, he may be too far gone. In order to do that, I must be adamant that I am not to be undermined. The situation with Ann is indicative of the continual undermining I suffered and the lack of courage displayed. Part of why I gave you that freedom was because I realized that if you would not set me free, I had to run away and seek my own freedom.

My way with words could deceitfully get me another woman, but that could never touch the love I have for my son. However, that love can't just be cosigning; it has to have flipside to it. I need him to embrace the fact that we are in it together, and that if we have a problem, we can work through it, not just point fingers. I was never able to accomplish that with you, but to accomplish it with him means I must go through you. I don't like that prospect, because I've set myself free from you.

So for me to return to Brian through you, I will only do it through a side-by-side focus on Brian, with dialogue serving as a go-between. I will die before I let another situation like the one with Ann occur. That profits nothing. That said, you must read one more document in order to move me even closer to the mutual object of our desire: Brian."

Here is the second letter:

"Eighteen months ago, I began an all-or-nothing campaign to take back my life. I decided that I had to go for broke. That said, I knew that you like to straddle the fence and that even if you wouldn't let me in, I would have to let you go. I knew, no matter what, that unless there is courage to shift principles, I would forever be stuck in a minimalist, trivial, tit-for-tat, accusatory dance. Now, just imagine if I'd come back in October — would the underlying issues have been dealt with on a consensus basis with all that defensive posturing? At least you have my so-called failures as corroborating evidence to justify your mindset.

Despite that, we were starting to make strides, but you never really let me in because you couldn't get over yourself. There were always string attached, and thank

God there was always something to point to in order to back up this mindset.

For too long, you put distance between us through a checklist mentality and by looking for corroborating evidence to confirm your suspicions, uncertainty, and fears. The reason I say that it is a matter of courage is that I let you go and let you in, something you never did for me. I don't bring that up to play tit-for-tat but to create peace. If you read my essay and give me an honest assessment of its principles, then it will move us a little closer to peace. If not, it shows me that you haven't really changed despite your pretending. It's time for you to be benevolent; that's the least you owe me for the freedom I gave you, which you weren't willing to give me."

Struggling Souls

I don't have to be James Brown to sing out loud, "I got soul!" We all have soul. However, life throws physical, mental, emotional, and other challenges at all of us. We all have drawbacks and downfalls that mightily challenge us. The challenges plant themselves in the depths of our heart; if they are uprooted, we will have a lifetime of adjustments to struggle through.

There is always going to be a darkness of despair that stirs up fear in us. I came to this stern realization as I tried to put my marriage back together. I had to do some soul-searching to realize that our behavior reflects our childhood. Coming to terms with that reality left me a little bristled with fear, but before long, I was empowered with hope and the confidence to overcome.

I have to share this with you because human beings express their desires, feelings, and inclinations. We must all grasp that, because it is a reconciling truth. Not to get too technical, but to really hone this point, let me share this: Emote is an intransitive verb which means that it doesn't take on a direct object until prompted. Nor does it transition into a transitive verb until it is reordered within the context or confines depending on the motive of the object. Thus, it becomes active or emotive. It changes form or shape when shifted to its environment. A person may act differently depending on their situation, motives, desires, and the root of those motives and desires.

What is the subterfuge (activity intended to misrepresent something's true nature)? What is behind what we see on the surface? What are our innate, intangible desires? Which runs our life: fear or faith?

The more I came to apply these principles to my life, the more my life was transformed. The transition was my struggle; I am sure that it is yours, too.

It's Just Me and You

Searching for the right answers to life's problems is like playing chess; you are certain that you made the right move until someone counters you with, "Check."

In my late twenties and early thirties, at times I felt stranded on a lonely highway. I wondered if I was meant to always be puzzled. Maybe life had no clear-cut answers.

Only when I decided to walk by faith did I gain a strong sense of purpose. I realized that the 'evidence of things hoped for' requires you to go counter to the notion of 'I'll believe it when I see it.'

How does this affect you?

I hoped that my life's path would reveal itself as I grew from the inside out. I don't have to look heavenward to realize that wrongs can be righted. That is why I challenge you to take stock of your puzzlement. Is it your poverty, past hurts, or a failed or failing relationship? You are not alone. That sounds snooty and pretentious on the surface, but it's ruefully true.

Love Complicated

This bizarre email was written by a man to a married woman making unwelcome advances to him.

> "Let me break it down for you. I know you are married and I respect that. I like you physically but I love you spiritually. I know it's not lust, because I'm not even thinking like that. I guess it's about closeness, intimacy, and partnership. That said, I wanted to keep the doors of friendship open, but I wanted you to tip your hand, show your bent, and give some indication that you can confide in me.
>
> That's why I wanted so badly for you to call; it would indicate your mindfulness, willingness, and desire to secure your marriage. Acting with intent carries weight with me. I am about the text and subtext, the root and sub-root. I am not just about fruits; an apple doesn't just appear but comes from a seed. I love the whole organic process. I desire substance over style or form. For example, can you count your ex-boyfriends on one hand?
>
> I know it's complicated for you, and although I am putting some pressure on your situation, I don't want to come across as two-faced. I am fond of you, and I can serve in whatever capacity you would have me — friend, confidant, and spiritual advisor. However, you must tip your hand without expecting me to drop my pants or put my lips where they don't belong."

This puzzled me until I realized that he wanted her to think twice before she did what she planned to do. She later informed me that he kept metaphorically telling her that she had to crawl before she could walk. She wanted him to fulfill her in ways that her husband could not. She wanted him not just to listen attentively and securely but to shut up and make a move. When I probed further, she finally admitted that he had stated, "It's a bad move; you'd better think twice."

Love is complicated, as best reflected in "Complicated" by Avril Lavigne: "Why'd you have to go and make things so complicated? . . . You're acting like you're somebody else, gets me frustrated."

Always remember that although you are married, there will always be someone else whom you find attractive. That person can tempt you into compromising your marriage. Don't curse yourself or your wedding bed!

Courage

This endearing truth about courage really startles me: It allows an individual to approach difficulties and adversities head-on without fear holding them back. It includes boldness, determination, tenacity, and more. It allows you to stand up against your fears and overcome hindrances that threaten to diminish your capacity to fulfill your dreams and reach your goals.

Sometimes courage makes you go against the flow. If you profess a profound faith, it's more than becoming a zealot; it's about upholding your principles.

At some point, I had made up my mind that I was going to get back with him. I couldn't do right before God until I could overcome my fears. I etched into my mind the fact that courage, also known as bravery and fortitude, is the ability to confront fear, pain, risk, danger, uncertainty, and intimidation.

I Got the Power

> *"Power is the ability of A to get B to do something B otherwise would not have done."*
>
> Robert Dahl

My father was a complicated figure; his antics encouraged me to challenge my own assumptions and to arrive at my own conclusions. He challenged me in many wonderful ways; however, because he felt that my mother was steering me in a more conventional direction, he let go of our connection. I love him dearly and I wish he'd offered his counsel to me. A lot of his advice took root, even though I arrived at my own conclusion about God.

I always tried to give my daughter context. Her emotional life was very important to me. To this day, I have never known a love like I had for her. Yet, at the same time, my love for her father caused me to make compromises that, absent that love, I would've never made. Many times I thought he didn't deserve the marriage I have tried to preserve. Perhaps that's why I'm cautious now. Respect and fairness meant more to me than ever before, so I decided to reconnect with my husband.

Things Change

The Woman Warrior by Maxine Hong Kingston is more than a coming-of-age storybook. It invaluably shows how we all have to acculturate (adjust) to different environments. Some have an easier time than others. As the book chronicles, the ease of adjusting to a new environment depends on how one connects with the idea of doing so.

The narrator was born in the United States after her mother immigrated there. This led to a constant cultural clash between the two that horribly affected her assimilation. Going to a Chinese-American school didn't help matters much. Bizarrely, the mother saw all Americans as ghosts.

This sad tale highlights that being a foreigner can be incredibly challenging. See how our point of view can change us?

Chapter Seven

RECONCILIATION

"We must always change, renew, rejuvenate ourselves; otherwise we harden."

Johann

Wolfgang von Goethe

As my husband and I went through our reconciliation, I could not help thinking about how much is involved in the give-and-take process. We both had dirty laundry. His misbehavior goaded me and tempted me to trouble. Thank God, I was able to see our reconnection as more than wishful thinking. It helped me keep out of trouble and rise above our unclean past. In fact, because of our reconciliation, I put a special emphasis on straightening myself up. We both had to clean ourselves up.

I made a concerted effort to stop resorting to fighting to solve our differences. My curiosity ran amuck when I thought about how a family was properly managed. At times, I was overwhelmed when I thought about how much time I would have to give to others. I wondered if it would make me unhappy. I realized how precious time is and how you have to budget it wisely. The more I peered into the lives of others, the more I realized that we all have to divert crises sometimes.

Many, including our families, said we wouldn't make it. Some even declared that it was just a matter of time before we failed again. We were wise enough to agree that time would tell, but we both knew we played a vital part in the on-going process.

Does the same hold true for you? Are you the type that sees everything strictly from your own point of view? Can you see *it?* Do you recognize that *it* is bigger than you? Although you are involved in *it,* others are, too. Even if you weren't involved in *it,* others might be. That's the beauty of reconciliation. It allows you to get a grip on how you relate to others and what part you play in *it.* That alone is worth reconciling.

The Power

After my husband and I had reconciled, I realized that some changes were desperately needed. I also realized that power is complicated. Still, I was well aware of the fact that I had the power to change myself — if I was willing. More than that, I realized that there is a constant push-pull dynamic when dealing with others. One does not obviate (make redundant) the other. Thankfully, I realized that God is greater than any problem I have.

I knew I had to be smarter and willing to facilitate (make easier) our ability to make ends meet. I realized that we had to organize our thoughts and make more sense of our environment. In other words, we had the fill the gap between knowing what to do and actually doing it.

That's not good enough when you become full of pride. When you fall down or are pushed down, how do you come back? I'm thankful to fully understand resiliency, the ability to bounce back successfully when troubles come and to seek and utilize resources in order to solve problems.

For the life of me, I can't understand how I was able to resist fighting back, getting in the last word, or saying, "I told you so." I was enlightened and wanted to be a good wife, but I was in the best of times and in the worst of times. Putting God first epitomized my transferring power. It was a change that had my emotions in a tug-of-war. I was hoping that, by the grace of God, I wouldn't have to resort to something I would woefully regret. I was hoping that my husband would fully recognize that we could achieve order together.

Balancing power is easier said than done. If you've ever had someone tell you, "You had better do as I say!" then you grasp the dynamic I was wrestling with during our reconciliation. I knew there had to be a balance or shifting of power. It was like an uphill battle. It makes me think of athletes in a triathlon. I'm bewildered by what possesses them to go through the ordeal of each seemingly impossible stage, but I use their perseverance as a guide. It helps me keep in mind that we get second and third chances.

The emerging reconciliation brought the realization that power is a dynamic force. I began to get a firm grasp on the fact that on a day-to-day basis, power was connected in all kinds of aspects in our lives: home, school, work, church, et cetera. Chiefly, it involved relating to other people and nature itself. It was key for me, considering all that I had been through. It was one of the more important learning lessons in the early days of our reconciliation.

It dawned on me that our ability to succeed depended on our ability to interconnect. That meant that we had to create better alternatives than simply declaring power. As well, it was a landmark time to challenge my self-esteem. Instead of speaking out against something that mattered, my goal was not to win power but to share it.

My empowerment was akin to the empowerment of women. The very word 'power' manifests itself differently to modern American women. It means projecting yourself as the man in the house, working without a man in the house, or working with a non-working man in the house. It means allowing kids to eat cheap foods and raise themselves. My goal has been power-sharing ever since our reconciliation; it means changing our minds to understand that equality doesn't mean conformity but that we are better off than we were before. The dynamics of power have many indicators beyond equality. Gaining more information and control over our lives makes us more responsible. That invariably gives us more power.

Mind and/or Body

Sometimes when we go through adjustments, it costs us to make them worthwhile. Amid my reconciliation with my family, it hit me that the true cost of marriage is give-and-take. I found myself fighting indifference. This was an apt moment to be reminded that extraordinary feats can be accomplished. The most extraordinary connection I wanted to make with my husband was on a mental level. I figured that since we saw our past mishaps as an opportunity to rekindle, then we could take our reconciliation beyond an abstract hope.

Admittedly, my husband was neither the pillow of grace nor the blanket of mercy, yet I was aware of the fact that we were uniquely united. Consequently, I constructed this poem as self-memorandum. It was directed toward my husband, yet it reflects an ongoing piece of fruit:

> Can you stimulate my mind — and not just my body?
> Can you stimulate my mind — and not just my body?
>
> I'm so much more than a pretty face.
> God birthed me with a dream.
> Momma always told me, "Be careful who you love
> —   things aren't always as they seem."
>
> Momma also told me that my body is a temple
> And to take good care of it while young,
> "Little girl, please! Don't try to grow up too fast!
> You'll just wind up getting stung!"
>
> Can you stimulate my mind and not just my body?
> Can you stimulate my mind and not just my body?
>
> You must remember: What looks good to the eye
> May not be good for the heart.
> You were born to love, lead, nurture, and provide.
> It was God's intention from the start.
> Instead of being frightened by the snapshots in your mind,
> Manifest the dream that's in your heart
>
> Can you stimulate my mind and not just my body?
> Can you stimulate my mind and not just my body?
>
> Never chase a fantasy, but always follow your dreams.
> Momma always told me, "Things aren't always as they seem."

I Don't Know

As time went by during our reconciliation, I wanted to put everything into perspective. I wanted us to be more than a church couple. I wanted to apply the Gospel to our lives. I knew that as long as I unafraid of the unknown, then we could make it through our uncertain future. A change in attitude was needed urgently; I knew that we lived in a world of uncertainty. People use 'I don't know' so much that it'll never go out of style in a hundred years. My gargantuan problem is that people say it with so much certainty that I wonder if they even realize what they are saying. Going through what I went through, I knew that transformation was an opportunity to seize, and I felt like they were denying themselves.

Equally, I knew that my recovery wasn't going to be an easy road, but I was ready to go down it, no matter how bumpy and rocky it was. I realized that it was a must-do. How could I hide behind 'I don't know'? I was certain that under the right leadership, we could stymie a lot of opposition and rebuild our lives. However, I had to move beyond being a 'why me' person. Proving things to oneself is always fundamental to development. I felt like a spark of the divine was within me; my job was to light it.

One pet peeve I have about 'I don't know' is that it's defeating. As a firm believer, you know that you must overcome self-alienation. Also, it's disturbing and can keep things lopsided to the point of making you one-sided. Really, there is a point between victim and victimizer. From my understanding, that is a middle ground many people don't like in this either/or society.

Sometimes a person won't be there to commiserate with us, so we won't receive our fair treatment. The beauty of taking off your blinders is that it makes you accountable. Your self-worth becomes tied to others. You see a value in giving rather than receiving (as incredible as that seems). You are worth waking up to the truth rather than denying it. I know that for sure.

Don't Front! I Got You Open

In New York City, they say, "Don't front! You know I got you open." The speaker knows who you really are; you can't pretend to be something you are not.

There were many times when I tried to put on a brave front, as if I had it all figured out. I tried to act vengeful when the time felt right. I thought my behavior would be validated through anger and rage. Yet I was wrong on all counts, and something was vying for me to quit pretending.

There was a man whose son had died in a neighborhood squabble. The man, an ardent believer, did not outwardly express his grief; he simply told people that his son had gone home. At the funeral, he said the same thing. However, at the burial site, he stared at the coffin, shaking his head in disbelief. All of a sudden, he threw himself onto it and cried out, "God, how can you take my son? Why did you let him die?"

Then an inner voice said to him, *"I took my own son, too. It was time."* The man retreated back to the well-wishers and accepted their expressions of sympathy while putting on a brave front. Yet people noticed that he seemed displaced. Later on, he acknowledged that although he was there, he was somewhere else at the same time. He was like a glimmering star. He was in rarified air, hiding and abiding in the secret place of the Almighty.

I understand this story very matter-of-factly. Although the situation is different, it relates to my own situational experiences. I could bring up a laundry list of grievances and go on and on about the wrongs done to me, all while ignoring my own wrongdoing. But that would not provide me the privilege of dwelling in the secret place of the Almighty, as that tender-hearted father learned.

Today, I cannot pretend or front. I have been opened by His truth, that I can abide in that presence. For that blessed reason, I don't have to front. What about you?

Stress

Almost from the beginning, I knew that something was wrong with my marriage. I didn't quite know how to express it, but I could clearly see that something was wrong. We went our separate ways until we decided to reconcile. However, after we reconciled, we took it upon ourselves to begin the painful yet exhilarating task of getting our lives back together. We wanted to work on our life skills. For us, that meant learning how to cope with life's stressors.

Please bear in mind that stressors — any emotional or physical demand — affect everyone. I knew I had to make some fundamental changes in how I responded to whatever conflict came my way. I couldn't simply fly off the handle, blow my stack, tongue-lash, and so on.

I realized that I had to constantly work on my emotions — anger, anxiety, embarrassment, fear, pride — so that I didn't retaliate any more unfavorably than in the past. I decided to develop my life-management skills, especially to deal with conflict. In fact, the more I looked into others' lives, the more I realized that I had to work on mine. However, we first need to agree that our lives are filled with stress, judging by the way we feel when we react to pressure situations.

We live in a world of people, situations, and things. That knowledge alone can cause a fire to boil within. The point I don't want us to lose sight of is that this is very much an inside/outside dynamic. We have to constantly learn to respond to the three types of stress: acute, episodic, and chronic.

Acute stress is a short-term stress which, in times of danger, causes the body to react or defend itself from everything, from large crowds to insect bites. Acute stress comes on suddenly but disappears quickly.

Episodic stress occurs during certain life periods, especially the adolescent years, due to peer pressure, parental pressure, and life adjustments. It is manageable, but it can have long-term consequences. Some of the mistakes made during this time make you pay for the rest of your life.

Chronic stress is the most nagging, because it deals with constant or ongoing situations involving family, school, relationships, jobs, and so on. This type of stress can wreck us physically and mentally.

The stress points are divided into normative and non-normative stress. Normative stress, like relationship issues and grade anxiety, are caused by events that are expected to occur. Non-normative stress, like serious illness and family divorce, are caused by events that are not expected to occur.

We need the right infrastructure in our lives to facilitate growth. For me, it included learning to recognize when I was in a tense atmosphere. I made a firm declaration in my mind that I would learn to adjust to conflict by seeking out workable solutions. When the winds of change blew in, I had reasonable expectations that I could adjust accordingly. I knew I had the power to respond effectively to what life threw at me. I knew that at the moment of decision, I wanted to tap into more than emotion. Over time, I became a cool-headed person. I also learned that I had a lot of control over what I would and would not subject myself to in a variety of situations, circumstances, and events.

Is Your Boat Right?

June Boatwright is the touchstone character in Sue Monk Kidd's novel, *The Secret Life of Bees*. She is a struggling soul and appears to be a rude and crude person, but her fear of commitment and inability to deal with things honestly gives you the idea that something in her heart tells her that this isn't right. Her reluctance and trepidation about stowing away a runaway adolescent girl brings her darkness to light. This character brings up a question for all of us: Can we get ourselves connected?

Like you and I, June struggles mightily to deal with herself. Her internal struggles come to mind when a situation challenges us. For instance, when things don't go as June plans, she retreats to her room. To isolate herself, she locks the door. To console herself, she plays her cello. Yet is she dealing or reeling?

To indemnify this character flaw, the apparent runaway comments, "I wish June with her whip would grin, too, but she only look[s] annoyed." Obviously June's normal is not-so-normal at all. Beyond being easily peeved, she appears unable to adjust and deal with change.

June embodies a fear of commitment, probably because she was scorned by a would-be husband who never showed up on their wedding day. That jolt not only left her heart-broken, but it gave her ironclad assurance that she would never make that mistake again. It makes her repeatedly turn down another admirer named Neil.

To explain not wanting the runaway to live in her house, she proclaims, "She's White." Clearly, June is a woman who not only must go through life-altering situations, but she must make proper adjustments. Thankfully, she does, and it aids her in becoming a loving and caring woman. She struggled through her internal strife to change her external circumstances.

Her character reflects real people. She shows how someone who has gone down the wrong path in life can turn around and find the right path. She found who she really was and what she really cared about. I'm sure the same holds true for you and me.

Closing the Gaps

The more my family reconciled, the more it became clear that we all needed to make adjustments. I did not want any longstanding family feuds, because I knew we had many skeptics. Instead, I wanted to learn how to close the gaps, and again, I received help from others. This excerpt was shared by a family who had reconciled while knowing that they had to put broken pieces back together:

The Father's Job Description:

- To cast the collective vision of the household
- To huddle with the family to coordinate and execute plans
- To learn new skills and train the family
- To coordinate family finances with the wife
- To make sure the children are meeting their goals
- To ensure that the family is progressing toward its desired destiny
- To ensure that everyone is participating in the overall development of the household
- To create special events for the children that will stretch their capacity
- To initiate discussions to close the gaps in the problem areas

The Wife's Job Description:

- To work closely with her husband to provide support, advice, and training to the family
- To maintain the household by paying the bills
- To maintain her feminine qualities at all times
- To support her husband's initiatives for the betterment of the children
- To support her husband's performance by identifying his problem areas and empowering him
- To assist her husband in assigning the division of labor

The Children's Job Description:

- To work closely with their parents to complete all tasks in a timely manner

Family Spiritual Goals

- To seek God through authentic worship and personal discipleship
- To serve others through giving and action

Dad's Goals

- Keep God first
- Be proactive in all areas
- Keep fit
- Focus on expanding business activities
- Reassess worthy projects
- Make time for recreation

Children's Goals

- Share problems and concerns with parents
- Team up with parents to maintain a clean and positive household
- Advance into his future by working on deficiencies
- Recognize when he's in over his head
- Surrender his will to God and family

Everyday Activities

1. Get up within fifteen minutes of alarm
2. Individual daily prayers
3. Coordinate bathroom times in a orderly fashion
4. Leave for work with the anticipation of arriving early
5. Clean up
6. Do daily clean-up after meals, with no food left in common areas
7. Put away clean laundry
8. Put things away where they belong
9. Sleep in nightclothes, not day clothes

Tidbits

These items vary by the family but can include ideas to make life easier for everyone involved, including possible scheduling conflicts, assignment of responsibilities, et cetera.

Chapter Eight

BUILDING COMMITMENT

*"Human beings, by changing the inner
attitudes of their minds, can change the
outer aspects of their lives."*

William James

The Half That Hasn't Been Told

Human history is full of imbalance. Women have a more vital role now than ever before. I'm not saying that equal rights and justice should make us domineering, but I am saying that we have more control than is realized, let alone advertised.

I'm not proclaiming that we are equally as strong as men, but ours is not brute strength. For example, ask a man if he's willing to have a baby and watch his body language. He will visually reinforce his response. This shows that communication is meant to express our feelings, ideas, and thoughts with others. In Latin, the word 'communicate' means to share. One of the important cogs in communicating effectively is listening, a skill that can make or break a relationship.

Listening

The powerful thing about reflecting on my adolescence was that it gave me some eye-opening truths. I saw that in my attempt to assume greater control over my well-being, I, like many others, involved myself in risqué behaviors, which could have been curbed if I had listened more attentively.

It's difficult to argue with people who fail to acknowledge the toll that listening takes in our lives, especially in these modern times. For example, there are many violent crime, detective, and police shows on television. They reveal how vital communication and listening are. Most people don't think twice about listening being a communicative tool. Yet watch a television show and see how listening serves as an integral part to any show, as though the producers know that people spend more time listening than talking.

Listening can be extremely beneficial to communication, but men and women listen differently. In general, women get a fuller meaning of the conversation by paying attention to body language, while men take words at face value. Men and women also process information differently. Men love to point to their stuff through achievements, trophies, et cetera, while women define themselves in terms of our connected feelings to people, places, and things. I could go on and on about this, but let us agree that both men and women can dodge questions. According to Colleen McKenna, these are respective needs for both sexes.

Men's Needs	Women's Needs
1. To feel accepted.	1. To feel validated.
2. To feel admired.	2. To feel respected.
3. To feel appreciated.	3. To feel understood.
4. To feel approved of.	4. To feel reassured.
5. To feel trusted.	5. To feel cared about.

I realized that my husband and I usually just talked instead of listening. I wanted and needed to change that, and over the years, we did.

Communication

The ability to communicate effectively without palaver (idle talk or beguiling speech) and lying is rare nowadays. However, I have grown and adapted to using communication to stand out in any occasion. First and foremost, my ability to read a situation and respond accordingly makes me sharp. I command respect through communication, to the point that I can make hardcore rappers apologize for portraying women as female dogs. I could be a hostage negotiator or crisis counselor.

I strove to put my best foot forward by reflecting on my past. Although initially overwhelmed, I possess recovery skills and a malleable, conductive mind. I have totally immersed myself in learning things with a wide-angle approach and narrowing focus as time goes on. Being the inquisitive person that I am, I have looked for inspiration from the streets to the cosmos, bearing in mind the infinite variations in-between.

Of communication, 7% is words, 38% is tone of voice, and 55% is body language.

Before communicating with someone, please consider:

- Why they want to communicate

- With whom they wish to communicate

- Where and when the message could best be delivered

- What they want to communicate

- How they are going to communicate

Interpersonal communication

'Inter', meaning 'among' or 'between', is very representative of our lives. Normally, it is person-to-person and/or face-to-face conversations. It can also involve a group discussion. Either way, since it is not a one-way conversation, we will be incredibly enhanced by remembering it during our communiqués.

I highly value and praise interpersonal communication, because, over time, it became a touchstone between my husband and I as we reshaped our lives, and it allowed me to take stock of my communication with my husband.

I realized that my protocol for communicating effectively with my husband and others involved learning the difference between assertiveness and aggressiveness. I realized that by being assertive, I was meant to express my thoughts and feelings in an honest, open, sincere, and straightforward way. In contrast, I had to watch my aggression, which made me express myself loudly and angrily. The more I went through moments of distress, the more I realized that assertiveness was more productive.

Part 1: Conflict

I have offered a variety of touchstone elements that cause breakdowns in relationships. One worthy of special mention is conflict. I don't mean disagreement, indecision, stress, or other common experiences that may cause or be caused by conflict. Below is a living example that will provide valuable insight into the notion of conflict.

1. *Marcus and Cheryl are interdependent.* That is, each needs something from the other, and they are vulnerable if they don't get it. Marcus needs to view landscapes to get an idea for an upcoming project, but Cheryl doesn't like the fact that he likes to do it on Saturday morning, the day they deemed their shopping day. Marcus proclaims that he cannot do his work unless he travels, but Cheryl complains that allowing him to do so is making her think about other men.

2. *They blame each other.* They find fault with each other for causing the problem. Cheryl criticizes Marcus for threatening their marriage; Marcus tells her to leave if it will make her happy, because her bitterness is destroying his creativity. Obviously, the 'he say, she says' has them sleeping in separate rooms. Each tells their respective listeners that the other one is cramping their style.

3. *They are angry.* Marcus and Cheryl project angry body language toward each other. She shakes her head and rolls her eyes; he grabs his genitals and tells her that he doesn't need her. They both pretend to appear and act polite, if they are in the right setting. They try to physically mask their seething emotions so that no one will offer a viable solution. Even if one of their supportive listeners offers needful advice, they come up with a bevy of excuses as to why they cannot do this or that.

Part 2: Conflict and Negotiation

I showcased the above example because they never really learned to communicate. I'm not suggesting that they need Samuel L. Jackson to come in and play negotiator, but they need some help. Why? From my understanding, this is a couple that became star-struck in the third grade. They obviously have some natural chemistry. However, life tests what they have and don't have. Apparently they lack communication. Because conflict rears its ugly head, they prefer to place blame on each other. Instead of thriving in the spotlight, they deflect it onto one other.

There is still conflict in my life. I am always dealing with it on one level or another. It usually involves my own inner conflict. Outside of me, it involves friends, family, and co-workers. Interestingly, I am not disdainful about this, although it tries my moods. Because I have my own past to reflect upon and extract from, I am able to present myself as a valuable asset to others, namely by being a listening ear or selective go-between.

Conflict will always be in our lives. We have to live with it and learn from it. Learning how to effectively negotiate with others will suit us well. We need to learn to adopt a good negotiation style to handle all the conflict that will come our way. This is essential because we constantly interact with others. Realizing that, I explored the idea of negotiation closer than ever. Let me share vital points with you.

1. Win-Win – This is the most ideal; both sides win.

2. Win-Lose – This is a powerful dynamic where one wins and the other loses.

3. Lose-Lose – Neither side gets their needs or wants met.

4. Draw – No outcome; they couldn't reach a conclusion.

As you can see, whether it's business or personal, there is still that constant push/pull theme that makes its presence felt in our lives.

Silent Treatment

Less popular than Dracula but a bigger monster is the silent treatment. It is an ultra-powerful force in personal relationships. It is not a classic sign of abuse, but it is destructive nonetheless. It causes grief and severe emotional disturbance if left untreated.

Most people don't talk it through; they decided to walk away to cool off and take a deep breath, or they just ignored each other altogether. It struck me that their silence can make each other critical. It's also a way to exercise dominance. Both sexes can play this role.

It makes the receiver suffer a sense of loss and makes them feel unworthy. Wow! That alone is thought-provoking. Our situation was utterly different but equally valid. Although I was not prone to giving the silent treatment, I realized that it was another avenue I could go down. It was something that I had to keep in mind and that I beseech you to, as well.

Commune

When we commune (converse intimately; exchange thoughts and feelings) with a loved one, we need to advocate fair play. It's easy to point the finger and say:

1. You didn't turn off the television.

2. You didn't listen to me.

3. Your plans won't work.

Now, let's transform those statements:

1. I think you didn't turn off the television.

2. I thought you didn't listen to me.

3. I'm not sure your plan will work.

It's easy to dismiss this type of talk as high-minded chatter. However, we have to level the playing field and make things more interactive rather than 'me versus you'.

Gossipmonger

I was floored upon hearing the term 'gossipmonger', a person given to gossiping and divulging personal information about others to hurt them. It struck me that many of my close associates, as well some members of our family, were prone to gossip.

The gossip dogged my steps. I saw that my past conduct gave people the ammunition to shoot fire at me, and even though the information was often misguided, it allowed people to pull others in and around them. My past character created an opportunity for them to assassinate it. That sounds harsh, but I knew I had an uphill battle.

Back when my husband and I were separated, the gossip hardened me. I felt emotional pain. It caused division and filled me with spite. It embarrassed me. It was destructive in many ways.

On the flipside, as I was reconciling with my family, I stayed mindful of how destructive gossip can be. Even more than that, I cringed and sighed before saying, "You reap what you sow."

I decided to be constructive by not being a gossipmonger. Also, knowing how providential it was, I adorned myself with

Psalm 19:14: "Let the words of my mouth and the meditation of my heart be acceptable in Your sight, O Lord, my strength and my Redeemer."

I also held near and dear to my heart Psalm 91:1-2: "He who dwells in the secret place of the Most High shall abide under the shadow of the Almighty. I will say of the Lord, 'He is my refuge and my fortress; my God, in Him I will trust.' "

Despite what others said, thought, or felt about me, I knew that God would protect me from all hurt, harm, danger, and from the people who were slandering my name and character.

Crisis Is Opportunity

I was steadfast in my determination to right my wrongs. Thank God, I knew I was not alone. A woman who had spoiled her kids shared this note with me. It was from her second husband, who married her because he valued her as an effective listener.

> "I wish you would have taken more interest in trying to help Laura help herself. Even though they weren't my children, I wanted to help them help themselves. I have heard her and Lance spew their hatred and disdain for you, not for what you do for them but for what you don't do. They want complete freedom.
>
> Just to show you how thoughtful and considerate I have been without respect or due credit, I'll give you a copy of the stuff that Laura leaves behind routinely. She mocks you for even scolding her and for not being smart enough to figure it out. And instead of seeing the compassion I have bestowed upon her, she vilifies me for suggesting she talk to you or others.

I went downstairs last night and saw her doing one of her sneak tips. She put her clothes back together as if they had been off and she had been using the videocam to showcase herself. I asked her to respect herself. I accept that I have been labeled a monster in this mishap, so why continue to persecute me?

It's bigger than me. Believe me when I tell you that she and Lance know what to say when they want something. I've seen them both play coy, only to brag about it later. Don't forget that we have a daughter named Marissa. If you don't believe me, believe God!"

This shows me that to go from crisis to opportunity, you do have to see crisis as opportunity. It is like a burning bush moment.

Gaslight

The phrase, 'to gaslight,' means to deliberately drive someone insane by manipulating their environment and tricking them into believing that they have gone mad.

In the old play *Angel Street* (the movie adaptation of which was called *The Gaslight),* a man tries to trick his wife into thinking she is crazy by doing things and denying that they ever happened. The story supposes that when life throws you unexpected twists and turns, you start to question your sanity.

The lady, Paula Anton, played by Ingrid Bergman, thinks she's losing her mind, especially when she loses a broach given to her by her husband Gregory Anton, played by Charles Boyer. When she hears footsteps overhead (actually him) and sees the gaslights dim and brighten, she fears for her sanity. She finds it hard to deny reality, but her deceitful husband tries to convince her that she's seeing and hearing things. Thankfully, a Scotland Yard detective becomes aware of the ruse and helps bring the beguiling husband into captivity.

This story is unforgettable in many ways. It shows me that sometimes our clouded judgment is just a gaslight.

Similarly, the value you have is the value you place. No matter what happened in the past, there would be no gaslights that deceived me.

The Emotional Competence Framework

When we let our emotions get in the way of our thinking, it can have consequences on our decision-making processes. One might make a decision without thinking it through due to their emotional state. Bear in mind how this framework is central to our lives:

Personal Competence

These competencies determine how we manage ourselves.

Self-Awareness (Knowing one's internal states, preferences, resources, and intuitions)

- Emotional awareness: Recognizing one's emotions and their effects

- Accurate self-assessment: Knowing one's strengths and limits

- Self-confidence: A strong sense of one's self-worth and capabilities

Self-Regulation (Managing one's internal states, impulses, and resources)

- Self-Control: Keeping disruptive emotions and impulses in check

- Trustworthiness: Maintaining standards of honesty and integrity

- Conscientiousness: Taking responsibility for personal performance

- Adaptability: Flexibility in handling change

- Innovation: Being comfortable with novel ideas, approaches, and new information

Motivation (Emotional tendencies that guide or facilitate reaching goals)

- Achievement drive: Striving to improve or meet a standard of excellence

- Commitment: Aligning with the goals of the group or organization

- Initiative: Readiness to act on opportunities

- Optimism: Persistence in pursuing goals despite obstacles and setbacks

Social Competence (How we handle relationships)

Empathy (Awareness of others' feelings, needs, and concerns)

- Understanding others: Sensing others' feelings and perspectives and taking an active interest in their concerns

- Developing others: Sensing others' developmental needs and bolstering their abilities

- Service orientation: Anticipating, recognizing, and meeting customers' needs

- Leveraging diversity: Cultivating opportunities through different kinds of people

- Political awareness: Reading a group's emotional currents and power relationships

Social Skills (Adeptness at inducing desirable responses in others)

- Influence: Wielding effective tactics for persuasion

- Communication: Listening openly and sending convincing messages

- Conflict management: Negotiating and resolving disagreements

- Leadership: Inspiring and guiding individuals and groups

- Change catalyst: Initiating and/or managing change

- Building bonds: Nurturing instrumental relationships

- Collaboration and cooperation: Working with others toward shared goals

- Team capabilities: Creating group synergy in pursuing collective goals

Chapter Nine

DISCOVERING YOURSELF

"The same people that politics separate, music makes them all gather around."

Anonymous

Spiritual Oneness

It will seem painfully untrue when I proclaim my husband and I as spiritually one. However, we only became one when we decided to place our trust in God before each other. It allowed us to not abuse our power.

Yes, we have been at odds and were once severely out of balance and seemed unmatched. Still, when we profoundly realized that our strange lessons were only complimentary fragments, we realized that two could become one.

Renewed, we attached the phrase '*United We Stand, Divided We Fall*' to our souls. Combined with our other elements, we became endowed with spiritual oneness.

Maybe your oneness is in another vein. If so, don't allow outside forces to divide and conquer you.

Destiny Killers

"Destiny is no matter of chance. It is a matter of choice. It is not a thing to be waited for; it is a thing to be achieved."

William Jennings

We must go after our destiny if we want it to happen. Everyone has a destiny, but the choices we make today are the deciding factors in what paths our lives will take. Destiny is accomplished piece by piece. By reconciling my family together, I was ready to take lessons from a variety of sources.

One source worthy of special mention is *A Tree Grows in Brooklyn* by Betty Smith, in which a girl named Francie Nolan leads a hardscrabble life. Even though her family is poor, she and her brother make a concerted effort to get a good education. Her unemployed father drinks his blues away, but rather than disown him, she becomes a living example of how actions speak louder than words. She is well aware of the shame and disappointment her father's antics bring to them, but she loves him nevertheless. She decides not to let it be a destiny-killer but to learn from it. She lets her father serve as a constant reminder of why she is not going to indulge in alcohol and lets it galvanize her to get a solid educational foundation. Her destiny is to get the education that her father did not have.

Moreover, Francie's quest to have a better life and the choices she made decided her destiny. That shows me how our choices affect our destiny. Most of us don't know our destiny until it happens, but when it does, it challenges our resolve. In many ways, it is a stimulus and response motif. As you go through life, the judgment you use to make choices will leave an imprint on your fate. Marriage, college, career, and family all weigh heavily on your destiny. The discoveries you make through your experiences and those of others help you gain perspective. This newfound perspective, like the one Francie gained about drinking, will help you make decisions that affect your destiny.

Lastly, Francie's story shows that there are many destiny-killers out there. Surprisingly, we might be one of them. At best, we foresee others as killing our destiny. At worst, we don't foresee that we are killing our own destiny.

For example, there is a young lady in Florida who would rather spend her time club-hopping and getting tattoos than actively seek her future. Her tagline is, "Don't hate the player; hate the game." I pray that she will find out that life has more in store for her. I know it did for me.

Are you a destiny killer or a dream maker?

Character

Sow a thought and you reap an act;
Sow an act and you reap a habit;
Sow a habit and you reap a character;
Sow a character and you reap a destiny.

—Charles Reade

The experiences I gained from attending different spiritual and self-efficacy meetings helped me make moral and responsible decisions that will guide me in life. These experiences, accompanied by the support and encouragement of my family, have molded me into a more responsible citizen, a reliable friend, and have improved my ethics.

I first needed to define what good character is and set clear goals. I found that good character consists of knowing good, desiring good, and doing good. I feel that these are the same goals parents have for their children. The problem can stem from the parents not having a real grasp of what these three goals mean.

Who You Are

Who you are must be bigger than what you do. At the same time, what you do will reflect back on who you are. I bring up the following character chart to reflect real people who live all over the United States.

Character	Kind of conflict experienced	Cause of the conflict	Response of this person	Consequences for this person
David	-Social/political - Conscience - Interpersonal - Economical	-Loves to flirt -Hates politicians -Hates the value of working, instead, prefers to live off of others	-He knows that women love iconic characters, so he tries to look as much like Brad Pitt as possible -Violent toward Paris	-He is hated by men and coveted by women

Almira	-Interpersonal -Economical	-Hates talking to women	-Denies that anybody can take David from her -Loves to work two small-paying jobs	-Kids live with their father
Lisa	-Social/political -Interpersonal	-Upset that her two sisters have better-looking husbands	-Blames her parents for mistreatment because she was the middle child	-No interaction with her sisters
Tasha	-Social/political -Conscience -Interpersonal	-Hates all women without tattoos -Hates to vote -Loves to be right	-Loves to call people 'haters'	-Constantly involved in verbal banter with adversaries

Do any of the above people remind you of yourself?

Shaping Identity

No one else in the world thinks, feels, or acts the way you do. These qualities that distinguish you as a person and differentiate you from every other person make up your identity.

We are what we have been persuaded to be by our families, culture, gender, friends, teachers, and significant others. How we feel, think, and act is attributed to both nature and nurture. People reinvent themselves all the time because they are trying to get a firm sense of their identity. I'm sure you can think of many examples where people act in accordance with their perceived identity.

Our lives often become topsy-turvy when the way we are is out of sync with the way others perceive us. Many of us wrestle with this because we all put ourselves in situations or roles which demand that we display a different identity.

We are most comfortable when being ourselves. We are upset when our thoughts, feelings, and actions are not in harmony with the person we think we are. We are also upset when we are cast in situations or roles that demand behavior inconsistent with our concept of ourselves.

Self-Image

Our self-image is the picture we have of ourselves. We learn about it at the earliest stages in our lives, when we learn to respond to the people who call our names.

As we grow, our self-images become more dynamic, shaped by our interactions with others, especially our closest associates. We learn to see ourselves as others see us and as we want to be seen. As time goes by, we are less susceptible to our environment and our interaction with others. This is when we can become a stranger to ourselves by hiding who we really are.

For example, here are some ways adolescence impacts us:

	When Adolescence Begins	When Adolescence Ends
Biological	Onset of puberty	Capable of reproducing
Emotional	Beginning of detachment from parents	Have a separate sense of identity
Cognitive	Developing reasoning abilities	Advanced reasoning abilities

Interpersonal	Shift from parental to peer relations	Develop intimacy with peers
Social	Training for adult work	Attainment of adult privileges and role
Educational	Entry into junior high school	Completion of formal schooling
Legal	Attainment of juvenile status	Attainment of majority (adult) status

Information gathered by Laurence Steinberge 1999.

Mission Impossible

We all have to sustain a miraculous coexistence with others. Unfortunately, situations will arise that threaten our ability to peacefully coexist. Worse yet, situations from our past can keep coming back. In my case, I have struggled with bonding with my mother-in-law. More than once, the mission has come to an impasse.

My mother-in-law and I were like the Hatfields and the McCoys; we routinely and repeatedly allowed past offenses to keep us apart. Because our lives did not intersect, we failed to see how devastating our actions were for each other. We held onto past grievances as if they were more important than God. We failed to realize that by having that mindset, we thwarted the personal true-love relationship that God wanted to have with the both of us.

The more I became attuned to the transformative power of the Holy Spirit, the more I allowed Him to give me a spiritual makeover. In other words, I was steadfastly being convicted of my wrongdoing. One day, as I sat in on a women's ministry group, we were reading *Deal With It!: You Cannot Conquer What You Will Not Confront* by Paula White.

I was convicted so strongly about my relationship with my mother-in-law and knew that I had to make things right. Upon realizing that the time had come, I went to her, forgave her, and asked for forgiveness.

It was a release, like Alka Seltzer! The thing that I had dreaded for so long, God made simple. When God releases us from something, He relieves all pressure! I see that my situation benefits many, but what about you? What situations are you living with that seem impossible to bear?

I had come down a long and winding road. I could chronicle a whole list of my offenses from my mother-in-law's perspective and vice versa, but for either of us to be right didn't matter. I knew that signing a peace accord is difficult if you won't negotiate your ironclad perspective. Give-and-take is more than just a buzzword.

Although you may feel as though you cannot forgive someone for a past offense, your earnest desire to have a right relationship with God must outweigh your grievances against any individual. Forgiving someone is not only for that particular individual; forgiveness is for you! Fantasia Barrino said it best: "Go ahead and free yourself!"

Lastly, we all find ourselves in desperate situations that test our resolve. Of course, our bonds must bend without breaking. When this strange realization comes to mind, we will be beside ourselves, yet we cannot let it stop us. Even if it comes across like an impossible mission, make it your mission, so help you God.

Right Place at the Wrong Time

The situation with my daughter is vastly improving, but I suspect that my past has returned. Something told me that life's journey begins and ends with you, although you are linked up with others along the way. On some level, that was just a philosophical musing; however, once my daughter got older, I could tell that the chickens were coming home to roost.

Her actions were God-awful. I'm not saying that it was destiny calling, but something told me that her antics would come back to bite me.

Just like myself at a young age, she was hardheaded, allowed herself to be manipulated, mimicked her peers' inappropriate behavior, and did things she knew were wrong and against what we were teaching her. It was saddening and very disappointing for me to see her travel down some of the same dark roads that I had, just for acceptance or to be liked by someone.

She thought that I was angry because of her actions, but it was also because I didn't want her to make the same mistakes that I had made, such as allowing a man to misuse her, play mind-games with her, mess her up, and cause more bad behavior.

Despite turning my life over to God, being unforgiving blocked me from truly understanding why Jesus had said, "Forgive them for they know not what they do."

I could often hear her murmuring about me and Hitler. Little did she know, I somewhat regretted scolding her. My spite was stronger, though, and communicated itself with a vengeance. It was by the grace of God that I didn't become violent, as well.

She, like me, was all too aware of how to maliciously navigate her way through people. This was frightening to me, because times had been different back when I was running. It's dangerous nowadays to be carefree and careless about whom we choose to associate with and what things we're going to participate in.

I was so good at encouraging others, lifting them up, and

reminding them of the grace that we Christians must extend. But when hell was dropped on my front step, God had to remind me once again of the grace that had been extended to me over the years and, in turn, which I had to extend to her. At that point, I started to talk openly with my daughter about the mental, physical, emotional, and spiritual ramifications of fornication. As someone once said, "One moment of pleasure can bring a lifetime of pain."

The Bluest Brown Eyes

This poem displays the disturbance of relationships.

This nameless young lady I knew
Had the prettiest brown eyes I ever did see,
One look and they would paralyze thee
These eyes were translucent despite the sparking glare
If you were not careful, you were bound to stare
And if you became fixated in a hypnotic daze
You would soon realize that her hazy world is like a complex maze
As you go down one path, it closes, forcing you to go down another
You wonder if you'll ever find your way out and should you even bother
Maybe, you think, I should start all over again
But once you're in, you're in to stay; no turning back, my friend
You're trapped in a danger zone full of confusion and doubt
Which way is up? Is there any way out?
Perplexed? Well, join the party
You've heard the saying 'misery loves company'
I've been trapped here for fifteen years
Not allowed out due to tears and fears
I'm not the only one here, I've just been here the longest
I've seen a few and heard of a few others
All terribly all in the same predicament

Bound by a struggling soul afraid to admit
There no reason for any of us to be here for this long
Are we all are a part of another sad love song?
With grief, I cry out, "Please let us go, Pretty Brown Eyes!
For if you don't, we will be your demise!"
We're still here, so I'm left to conclude
Those eyes might be beautifully brown on the outside
But inside they are miserably blue

Chapter Ten

THE TIME HAS COME

"Therefore, as we have opportunity, let us do well to all, especially to those who are of the household of faith."

Galatians 6:10

The Greek word *'kairos'*, meaning, 'the right time', encapsulates a large part of what I have been chiming throughout this book. It refers to the right opportunity to seize the moment.

Upon reading the writings of the Apostle Paul, I realized that he was imprisoned at various times. He seized that time to bring people into fruition and show them that God had changed his outlook. He was changed by recognizing the truth of his mission. He could draw closer to God by allowing himself to be changed. He found the opportune moment to show his inner change and relate it effectively to others.

Paul constantly seized opportunities to bring about the desired change in whatever venue that was in due season. Like Jesus, he went against the grain to bring about change. Like Nelson Mandela, he stayed in prison to change the system that had imprisoned him. Instead of getting out of prison to free himself, he stayed in prison to free others.

We can't relate to other people by pointing out how much better we are than them. We must understand their perspective and seize the opportunity to help them get to where they need to be. It's easy to be one-sided, but being two-sided makes us open to communication. It's an opportunity to be living proof that change is in order. An opportunity can be seized or missed. Therefore, understand that *kairos* is a season of opportunity.

What I've wholeheartedly tried to share is that I've been through various times in my life where I did not seize the opportunity for change. I was going through the *chronos* (Greek word for *time*) while missing the *kairos*. By and large, my most significant changes occurred in due season when I seized the opportunity to allow my life to be transformed from the inside out.

It included my marriage relationship, my church relationship, and the right relationship with my daughter. They didn't all come in the same *kairos,* but they came in due time. By seizing the *kairos,* change happened over *chronos.* For instance, I seized the opportunity when my daughter was twelve to bring about vital changes by the time she was sixteen.

My change occurred when I realized that the first enemy I had to deal with was myself. I had thought of myself like Paul: A delicate creature cruelly buffeted by the coarseness of life. Yet life kept me on the right mission until I seized the opportunity.

For example, I had an ambiguous relationship with my husband; it was prone to an inner war between love and hate. But even though I could have gotten a divorce, I decided to seize the opportunity for marriage.

As I alluded to about a million times in this book, it's easy to place blame. Even constantly going over the laundry list of wrongs done to you can harm you. As for my husband, father, and even my daughter, I discovered the true price of love: To give more than you can expect in return. Furthermore, when you understand that grace is unmerited favor, you will experience a great awakening and can seize the opportunity. The same grace that had been extended to me, I had to extend to others.

As I let my own light shine, I seized the opportunity to give others the permission to do likewise. The same can hold true for you.

My main drive is not to shove religion down your throat but to give you the wonderful delight of spirit and truth. Likewise, one of the premier themes or concerns the Bible screams is not just our choice but our intention. I can thankfully say that I am more forthright than ever to seize the opportunities when they arise. Some opportunities are more subtle than others. However, I seize the opportunity when the impetus propels me and discernment drives me to choose. The same can hold true for you.

Takes Only Time and Effort

Upon reflection, it is my strong belief that in order to achieve what you want, transcend a bad situation, or stand steadfast, it takes only time and effort, as my own story can attest.

I would be remiss if I did not add that life simply isn't fair. However, it is what you make of it through your time and effort. It isn't fair that the richest 1% in this country are wealthier than the poorest 60%. It isn't fair that people in Third-World countries are exploited and placed at a disadvantage to maintain the lifestyles of excess in First-World countries. It isn't fair that rich people face modernization while poor people suffer. Still, the world is predominately poor.

Besides the notion that life isn't fair, change is a constant force that pulls on us all. As surely as a child is born, he or she will die. We all have limited time on this Earth. But although change pulls at us, we often resist it. Most of us would rather wallow in our self-pity and selfish indulgences than to come into our own. All too often, our childhood has dire consequences that affect us as adults. This is usually when we turn to vices, such as stimulants, falsehood, or denial, to get through the day. Most of us simply do not grow into our own to resonate a constant positivism in our lives. Most of us can't even properly balance the negativity in our lives.

Interestingly, the woman who I am today is far greater than the girl I was just ten years ago. When I found Christianity and was called by God to serve Him, I gladly humbled myself and took up my cross. I slowly put my vices in check and began to let the newer "Me" emerge. I stopped fighting change. God didn't let me hate myself like a lot of us do. Even when the pressures were great, I humbled myself through God and held His space. I exercised my time and effort to have a positive effect on others.

Case in point, I recently heard someone comment on how people are like buzzards because they live off dead things. This statement provoked my spirit, because I realized that I, too, was a buzzard; At that time, I couldn't embrace the changes that had to happen in my life. I was on sinking sand, and so now I ask: How many of you will be on sinking sand when God calls your number?

I realized, "The empty can rattles the most." People who are so puffed up with selfish pride try to find excuses to justify their way of life. I didn't have enough faith. The Bible says that faith is the substance of things hoped for and evidence of things not seen. In a nutshell, I didn't have enough faith that the Almighty would work in my life because there were too many realistic and physical things that distracted me. However, it was the story of Jesus' death, burial, and resurrection that showed me that a lot of this life is a mystery. So many things are beyond our control that, to live in this uncontrollable world, we have to use our time wisely and exercise the proper effort to humble ourselves.

Life isn't fair; in fact, it's uncontrollable. I've seen so many complexities and grey areas in my life; it isn't as black and white as it should be! Still, we can take stock our lives. I am a living testament that you will grow weaker by neglecting to correct your faults. My life-circumstances gave me the confidence to say that he or she who seeks spiritual knowledge must first begin with humility.

Likewise, I realized that life is too short to be swallowed up by guilt, envy, pride, jealousy, or whatever else is holding you down. A friend once told me that I shouldn't judge a man unless I know his politics and what he's dealing with. I'm telling you, too, not to begrudge a person for something unless you know more about it. Before criticizing, first analyze what you don't understand.

I know that life gets hard at times and you don't know where to turn. You wonder if you should give up or persevere. I'm telling you that time is the master. It has no measure. That's why we should take it one day at a time. Still, keep in mind that in this uncontrollable world, change is possible. Remember that it takes only time and effort to know the righteousness of life.

As you trod in the valley of life, remember that life has consequences, not only while living but also after you die. In this world full of hate, love is the solution for life that will help us all get through. Love yourself enough today to let the memory of Jesus inspire you to look at your life.

With that, I say that the time has come.

360°

Sometimes we do a full circle 360° turnaround. For example, my father showed me what I showed my daughter: I can either tear you down or build you up.

While communing with my daughter, I learned that it's not what you say but how you say it. At first, I wanted to chastise her for being disrespectful. I voiced my displeasure, which made her roll her eyes and grit her teeth. I tried to convey my reasoning, since I could see myself in her. Naturally, this led to a war of words; I regret that I used my observations of her life decisions to attack her verbally. Unfortunately, my poor judgment and bad choice of words planted a seed of contempt in her mind. The more I hammered my point home, the more I seemed disrespectful. It was as if I was declaring my feelings without realizing how she felt about my feelings. Understanding that this was the point allowed me to open up my mind and think outside of the box.

She was me, and I was her. Until we came around on that point, we would constantly be at odds. The story of olive oil can reveal the beauty of this recognition. An olive is simply a tree's fruit, but when it is crushed, it becomes oil. By understanding this, I realized that beauty comes through crushing. This understanding helped me to curtail my communication with my daughter. Nowadays, I use my ability to communicate to bring about beautiful olive oil.

Double-A

We constantly make adaptations and adjustments in life. Some are more bearable than others. There will always be situations and circumstances that will force you to adapt and adjust. The adaptation will enlighten you.

For instance, someone went to Europe and had to adapt and adjust. Why? They had brought an electric hair dryer and curler. They were puzzled and weary when they realized that their equipment wouldn't work. Eventually, the hotel concierge informed them that they needed to get an electrical adapter to transform the American-sized current into a European-sized current.

Like it or not, we are malleable creatures. We are forced to make changes. Sometimes we make these adaptations and overcome. Sometimes we refuse and suffer the consequences. As a person who thought that love conquered all, I realized that I had to adapt and adjust to what love really was. I hope and pray the same holds true for you.

Emotionally Devoted To You

The machinations (scheming and conniving) of the heart run many things. Chiefly, it can make you avoid the self-scrutiny that we all have to go through. Yet, many of us don't do it when we blame others for our life choices. Unfortunately, I see why people think this way, but that doesn't make it right.

Similarly, I understand how paramount the quality of family and peer relationships can be in our lives. Be that as it may, there are many different virtues and values that need to be uplifted to maintain a healthy relationship. The one I am advocating beyond deep spiritual connection is emotional bonding.

I have contributed to relationships borne out of convenience rather than genuine affection. Their memories keep me humbled and allow me to participate in a better giving-and-receiving relationship with my daughter. This is time well spent. It's where I need to be.

But although I am in the right place, my daughter is not, at least for the moment. I want her to learn to take stock of situations until they are resolved, presuming they can and will be resolved. I want her to know that before you make big decisions, you need to step back from the current situation and look at what's happening a bit more objectively.

I encourage her and others; I know how we all put stumbling blocks in the way. It reminds me of the story of the prodigal son. He was living in abject poverty and utter despair until it dawned on him that he could simply return home. He had to be willing to remove the stumbling blocks of shame, disgust, and regret from his mind. Relationally, my daughter, or perhaps even one of you, can't see the required change in the foreseeable future, but it doesn't change the deficiencies which need to be adapted and adjusted.

The Redemption Song

I want to reinforce certain worthwhile notions such as forgiveness. Bear in mind, a natural extension of forgiveness is redemption. Sometimes there is a huge emotional chasm between you and a friend, lover, or relative.

On a relationship level, some couples rekindle sexually without reconciling relationally. The lack of commitment is twisted. They are more committed to sexual pleasure with each other than to satisfying themselves through a committed relationship. So, instead of disentangling from each other, they stay mixed up in a mess. Sex without commitments seems like heaven to a lot of people. I guess if there are six million ways to die, choose one. Some couples go separate ways because there is no remaining romantic spark and some remain only because of the spark. This doesn't strike me as redemption as much as misplaced priorities.

I implore you to be truly redeemed. Seek knowledge, wisdom, and understanding to help facilitate it. It will help you sing "Amazing Grace".

Revisited

Sometimes it gives me a sinking feeling when I think about how many relationships go astray over flings and walking on the wild side. That wild side can make you tie up your soul to people who aren't thinking twice about you; it can make your brown eyes blue, or your blue eyes black, if you catch my drift, especially if you hook up with a womanizing man.

I am brave enough to admit that I had intense passion for my husband in the first part of our relationship. Honestly, however, if I could have protected myself or fought against that passion, I would have. It is ideal to possess an eternal gratitude toward your mate. I have realized that we season our love-lives with a healthy dose of unreality. That's why I invited others to contribute so that you could see how widespread this debacle really and truly is.

Furthermore, several teachers contributed pieces throughout this book while wondering if I could give people the foresight to prevent future tragedies. I am primed and passionately driven to do so because I am a living testimony that it can be done. What a wonderful theme revisited.

Survival Story

This book could easily be called *Survival Story*, because it speaks of survival, especially complexes. Teenagers face a lot of complexes, with inferiority being the most dominant. Upon reflection, I realized that I suffered from it and that my response was the same: Overcompensation. I was ready to get cocky and act out if it meant I could get over.

The problem with this type of mentality is that it leads to teen pregnancy. According to http://www.preventeenpregnancy.org, 750,000 teenage girls a year get pregnant in the United States.

Shockingly, 73% of all teen pregnancies were not planned or expected.

Sex is not the end-all-be-all. Having a baby is not as blessed as it appears when you're a teenager. I understand that cultures all over the world have different viewpoints on this, but there are benefits to not having sex or a baby until adulthood. This is not a hypocrite talking but a person declaring to teenagers that they do not know the minute or the hour that conception will overtake them.

A mindful lyrical phrase by an '80s group called Heart is, "What about love? Don't you want someone to care about you?" These lyrics serenade me with the continual desire to have my soul complete with a beloved. According to the above site, the majority of those surveyed, of both sexes, wished they had waited until they were ready. This tells me that it's not something you go rushing into just to show how cool, hip, or down you are.

I know that unbridled sex looks fulfilling and that abstinence seems to kill teenage ambition. Believe me; you don't have to be a sex pistol to feel fulfilled. Your parents aren't square; likewise, parents, your teenagers aren't too hip. It's just a clash of inferiority complexes.

I know sex is a major issue for teens. I have endured and watched others endure pain for years. I proclaim myself as a survival story, not because I did or did not do all the right things but because of the grace of God. I could have fallen into complete disarray and disrepute because of the unwise choices I made concerning sex as a teenager.

I don't want people to blur the lines and do what they feel compelled to do as if they couldn't resist themselves. Don't get caught up; wise up. Survive.

Why Is That?

The glaring lesson that I had to learn and want to share is the concept of a soul-tie. In short, two become one. Biblically, it means that two souls become one flesh. It involves a classification in a biblical and non-biblical sense. In the ideal biblical sense, two become one when they are a married couple. "For this cause shall a man leave his father and mother, and shall be joined unto his wife, and they two shall be one flesh." (Ephesians 5:31)

In the biblical sense, the concept involves the spiritual realm. It taps into your belief and outright acknowledgment of being a soul inhabiting a body with a spiritual dimension. Understand that you are a body, soul, and spirit. The heightened dimension is the spirit. You can connect the body and soul without realizing that the spirit is still there in the mix. You can dismiss that as presumptuous, but the truth is supreme over all of us whether we acknowledge it or not.

Still, it leaves itself open to the question: Why is that?

In the most basic sense, Adam and Eve were really bonded by Eve being created from Adam's rib. God did the spiritual, soul, and physical surgery to make the one into two. He did it for a divine purpose. Likewise, He did it before mankind fell from its high position of grace, before sin was in the picture but while they had the option; therefore, when mankind fell, Adam and Eve fell together.

Interestingly, the vaunted connection they had was not only challenged by Satan, but it contributed to their downfall. As real as it went, Adam chose Eve's request to eat the forbidden fruit over God's declaration that if he did, he would die. He didn't die physically but was spiritually disconnected from God; this was repeated throughout human history.

Why is that?

We are fallen beings. Jesus is not called both the second Adam and the Redeemer for no reason. He came on a reconciliation mission. I am on one now. I share my story with you for the same reason Christ shared His in death: To redeem you.

Why is that?

It is because I know firsthand how a wicked soul-tie can impact your life. Frankly, it is fornication. More importantly, it is addictive mind-twisting that ties two souls together in the spiritual realm. In two spheres, there are godly and ungodly soul-ties. They both are pervasive, alluring, and can have a major impact on your life. The godly soul-tie is my top choice. I earnestly employ it because I know how someone's sordid past can prevent them from establishing a godly soul-tie.

I encourage you to not allow anything to keep you from meeting your Maker. That includes sex. There is a song that is embedded in my heart and spirit: "More Than Anything" by Lamar Campbell. Its powerful chorus goes, "I love You, Jesus, I worship and adore You; just want to tell You, Lord, I love you more than anything."Tie your soul to that.

Give Me A Reason

Let me mention a most valuable player on my team, my thirty-two-year-old sister. She is worthy of special mention.

As a preteen, it was always pretty cool to have this cute little face always smiling, looking up at me, asking me questions, and trying to mimic my style.

Although we grew up in the same house, I served as a valuable lesson for her. In a sense, I gave her a reason to go another way. Watching me go the wrong way on many occasions as we grew up spurred her to go the right way. Thus, she learned what not to do. She made a promise to herself not to follow my negative influence. She was a lot like Francie in *A Tree Grows in Brooklyn,* who was determined not to be influenced or taken advantage of by anyone who would cause her to act out the way I did during my teen years.

I think back on how I watched her walk across that stage to receive her college degree and how I held the train of her wedding dress (as she did mine), how I waited anxiously in the hospital nursery in the wee hours of the morning for her to give birth to my nephew, and how I watched her achieve so many other accomplishments. I remember that she did it all with determination, hard work, diligence, and dedication. It brings tears to my eyes to think of how her life and example has blessed me as I have allowed God to transform me.

Since I gave her a reason, let both of us give you a reason to change. By the grace of God, you will.

The Last Mile Of The Way

". . . *success is to be measured not so much by the position that one has reached in life as by the obstacles which he has overcome while trying to succeed."*

Booker T. Washington

Sometimes you just have to keenly listen to people when they speak. Sometimes we characterize it as their problem, not ours. It can indeed be someone else's problem, but this doesn't mean that it's not related to us.

I started to get a semblance of balance. I was concerned about whether I could find my way. Even worse, could I get there even if I got back on track? The ability to recover is viable. Without a doubt, it is a process that is filled with ups and downs. That's why the phrase 'even keel' is readily employable.

I'm not where I want to be, but believe you me, I'm almost there.

Role Models

Too often, these days, we get cynical. We just don't believe in much besides ourselves anymore. It's like we will never quit believing in ourselves. I don't mean to be crass, but no man or woman is an island. It sounds like pie in the sky, but you and I need role models.

I am not trying to belittle you, but I am still amazed by the concept of taking captive every thought and making it obedient to Christ. I know it's meant to be a biblical reference, but it is far more significant than that. It speaks to being locked in a particular frame of reference and humbly ceasing and desisting to take it in. Sometimes when you get locked in, it's as if you are in a zone. In this way, it doesn't make a difference if the thought is vicious; you can have it transformed, but only if you don't dwell on its negativity. Oddly enough, it completes you.

I have role models and mentors all around me. It's not necessarily a person who I see on a daily basis, but it's someone who leaves a firm impression on me. They serve as a guiding light through their reflective stories, personal experiences, et cetera. Sometimes they simply explain the ins and outs of a wide variety of things. This is integral, especially when you go through situations that bring these life lessons to mind, challenging you to think about what you would or wouldn't do.

Sometimes you think of the bigger picture. Sometimes your emotions try to be your ruler. Whatever struggles you go through, having a good role model or mentor will help quell your anxiety.

I really want you to take hold of this truth. It has a dynamic power embedded in it. Likewise, many echo this same sentiment. In his book, *The Audacity of Hope,* Barack Obama stated, "Democracy demands that religious Americans translate their concerns into universal values and secularists make room for faith and morality in the public square."

Lastly, whatever season or woe you are in, find a role model in whose benevolent spirit you can share. You can have an effective mentor who can serve as a guide to help you compensate from the residual effects that could last you a lifetime. Just remember the cost and consequences which I have shared with you. Call them a spiritual discount.

Au revoir from Tara

Intense, Intuitive, Spiritual, Thoughtful
Sibling of one individual
Who loves: Communication, Singing
Who needs: Communication, Knowledge, and Understanding
Who gives: Communication, Empathy, and Understanding
Who fears: Miscommunication, Ignorance, and Poverty
Teacher of Communication
Student of Life
Resident of the World
White